the story of Frederick Douglass

# CIVIL RIGHTS LEADERS

A. Philip Randolph

Bayard Rustin

Ella Baker

Frederick Douglass

Harvey Milk

Ida B. Wells Barnett

Roy Wilkins

W. E. B. Du Bois

William Lloyd Garrison

# unbound AND unbroken

## the story of Frederick Douglass

## MORGAN REYNOLDS
### PUBLISHING

Greensboro, North Carolina

## Unbound and Unbroken:
## The Story of Frederick Douglass

Library of Congress Cataloging-in-Publication Data

Esty, Amos.
Unbound and unbroken : the story of Frederick Douglass / by Amos Esty.
p. cm.
Includes bibliographical references and index.
ISBN 978-1-59935-136-0 (alk. paper)
1. Douglass, Frederick, 1818-1895. 2. African American abolitionists--Biography. 3. Abolitionists--United States--Biography. 4. Slaves--United States--Biography. 5. Antislavery movements--United States--History--19th century. I. Title.
E449.D75E85 2010
973.8092--dc22
[B]

2009054287


Printed in the United States of America
First edition

# Contents

Frederick Douglass
house in Washington,

# Chapter
# 1
# Born into Slavery

It took all morning for Betsy Bailey and her six-year-old grandson Frederick to walk the twelve miles from her small cabin on the Tuckahoe Creek to Edward Lloyd's plantation. It wasn't an easy walk for a young child, especially in the heat of August in eastern Maryland. The journey was also hard for Betsy, because she knew that she would have to leave him behind and return to her cabin without him, something she couldn't bring herself to tell Frederick.

Both Frederick and Betsy Bailey were slaves, although Frederick was still too young to understand exactly what that meant. He had been born in February 1818, but like many other slaves he never knew the exact date of his birth. In fact, for most of his life Frederick believed that he had been born in 1817. It was only when he was much older that he found out the actual year of his birth.

Frederick was owned by a man named Aaron Anthony, who worked as a manager on the plantation owned by Edward Lloyd. Frederick's mother, Harriet Bailey, was also owned by Anthony. She worked on a farm ten miles away from Frederick, and so she was rarely able to see her son. Instead, Frederick was raised by his grandparents, Betsy and Isaac Bailey.

Despite not having his mother around, Frederick was rarely alone as a child. His grandparents raised several of his cousins

A 1906 oil painting of Edward Lloyd

as well, so there were always children around to play with. As he grew older, Frederick gradually learned that he was a slave, and that his cousins and his grandmother were also slaves. Even the small hut—made of clay, wood, and straw—was owned by Anthony.

Growing up, Frederick heard everyone refer to his owner as "Old Master," and he learned that the man Anthony worked for, Edward Lloyd, was one of the richest men in Maryland. Lloyd had served as both a United States senator and as governor of Maryland, and he owned more than five hundred slaves.

So in 1824, when Frederick walked with his grandmother to Edward Lloyd's plantation, he had no idea why they were making the trip. When they finally arrived, Betsy told him to go play with the other children in the backyard. Frederick's brother Perry and his sisters Eliza and Sarah were among the children in the yard, although this was the first time Frederick met his siblings. Frederick didn't want to leave his grandmother and only reluctantly left her side. But instead of playing, he stood with his back against the wall, watching the other children. Before long, another child ran up to him.

"Fed, Fed, grandmamma gone!" the child yelled to Frederick.

Frederick, now worried, ran back into the kitchen. His grandmother was nowhere to be seen. She had left to make the long walk back to her cabin. Frederick was on his own.

As usual, the plantation was bustling with activity when Frederick arrived. Most of the slaves were at work in the fields growing wheat and tobacco, but others were blacksmiths, took care of the horses, tended the gardens, or worked as cooks and servants in Wye House, the mansion lived in by the Lloyd family.

Aaron Anthony, Frederick's owner and the manager of the plantation, was in charge of ensuring that everything ran smoothly.

When the slaves went out into the fields, they were watched by overseers, white men who were quick to punish any slave they thought wasn't working hard enough. The overseers reported to Anthony, and Anthony reported any problems to Lloyd.

When Frederick first arrived, he was still too young to join the other slaves at work in the fields, but he heard them talk about what it was like to be a field hand. The days were long, and the work was hard. On most days, work began at daylight and did not end until the sun went down. Only on Sundays were the slaves allowed time to themselves. There never seemed to be enough food, nor was there much time to eat what food they received. Instead of returning to their huts for breakfast, slaves would take food with them to the fields, often a small piece of bread made of corn meal. The slaves called these ash cakes, because they were cooked in the ashes of a small fire.

The Wye House in Talbot County, Maryland. This 1963 photograph shows the front view of the mansion, a National Historic Landmark. *(Courtesy of the Library of Congress)*

One day, Frederick heard a story that stuck with him for the rest of his life. While the slaves were out in the fields, the overseer, a man named Austin Gore, decided that one slave,

named Denby, wasn't working hard enough. Gore whipped Denby until the unfortunate slave broke away and ran into a nearby river, wading in until he was up to his shoulders to cool his bloody back. Gore yelled at Denby to return immediately, warning the slave that he would shoot him if he stayed in the water. Denby still refused to leave the water. Gore warned Denby three times. Each time, Denby stayed where he was. Then, Gore raised his gun and shot Denby, killing him. When Edward Lloyd later asked Gore why he had shot Denby, Gore replied that Denby had become unmanageable and was setting a bad example for the other slaves.

It didn't take long for Frederick to find out that violence was a constant part of life on plantations. Slave owners were always afraid that their slaves would rebel, so they tried to bully and frighten the slaves into submission. Many slave owners believed that it was their right to treat the slaves as badly as they wished. After all, they owned the slaves, just as they owned their horses, houses, and other property.

Sometimes Frederick witnessed this violence firsthand. Not long

11

after arriving at the plantation, Frederick was in the kitchen when he heard Aaron Anthony confront another slave, one of Frederick's aunts. She had disobeyed Anthony by slipping away during the night to visit a slave on another plantation, and Anthony caught her when she returned. Frederick heard them coming into the kitchen, so he hid in a closet. He heard his aunt scream as Anthony began whipping her. Frederick remained hidden until it was finally over, and he became afraid that he would be next. For the rest of his time on the Lloyd plantation, Frederick would occasionally hear his aunt being whipped by Anthony. Sometimes Frederick woke up to the sound of his aunt's screams.

Frederick was fortunate enough not to be whipped while living on the plantation, but he experienced many other difficulties common to slaves. For one thing, he no longer had his grandmother nearby, and his mother was too far away to visit very often. On the days when she was able to visit, he would fall asleep at night with her by his side, but he always awoke to find that she had left to make the long walk back to the farm where she worked. His mother never told him who his father was, although Frederick heard rumors that it might be Aaron Anthony or a member of Anthony's family.

Frederick's loneliness was made worse by a woman everyone called Aunt Katy. Aunt Katy was a slave, and she was in charge of the kitchen. If she liked a child, she would give him or her more food. But for some reason, she never seemed to like Frederick, and she never would give him enough to keep him from being hungry. One day, hungry as always, Frederick spotted an ear of corn sitting on a shelf in the kitchen. When he saw that no one else was around, he took it. He cut off some of the kernels and roasted them in the ashes of a fire, working quickly so as not to be caught. Just then, his mother entered the kitchen—she had arrived for another short visit.

When Frederick told her that Aunt Katy never gave him enough to eat, she was furious. She took a ginger cake and gave it to him, and then she found Aunt Katy and lectured her about treating Frederick fairly. That night, for one of the few times in his life, Frederick felt comforted. But as always, he awoke to find his mother gone. Frederick did not yet know it, but that would be the last time he ever saw his mother. She died when he was only seven, leaving him even more alone than before.

In addition to the constant hunger and lack of family, Frederick, like the other slaves, never had enough clothes to keep him warm in the winter. Every year, each adult slave on the Lloyd plantation was given two rough shirts, two pairs of pants, and a pair of socks and shoes. These thin, coarse clothes were expected to last the entire year, despite the constant wear and tear from all the hard work performed by the slaves. Like the other children, Frederick received only one shirt, and by the next winter it was more like a rag than a shirt.

As the weather got colder, Frederick tried to find ways to stay warm at night. He had no blankets, so he took a bag used for carrying corn and pulled it down over his head, leaving his feet uncovered. He got so cold that his skin cracked, and he spent the nights shivering on the ground of the cold clay floors of the hut.

Frederick's plight was similar to that of the 2 million other slaves living across the American South. Their conditions varied depending on where they lived and who owned them, but all were considered the property of their owners. They could be bought or sold, whipped or even killed by their masters.

Stirrup Branch Plantation, Bishopville, South Carolina, 1857
*(Courtesy of Civil War Photograph Collection, Library of Congress)*

Five generations of slaves are pictured in this 1862 photograph of a plantation in Beaufort, South Carolina. *(Courtesy of Civil War Photograph Collection, Library of Congress)*

The first African slaves in the New World were brought by Europeans in the 1500s to work in South America and on the Caribbean islands, where they toiled on sugar plantations and in gold and silver mines. European slave traders bought slaves along the coast of Africa and transported them on large ships to the Americas. Millions of Africans became slaves in the New World, and millions more died making the long journey across the Atlantic.

The English colony of Jamestown—the start of what would become the United States—was established in 1607. In 1619, just twelve years later, the first Africans were brought to the colony by Dutch traders. As the English colonies in North America grew, the number of Africans increased as well. But for the next few decades, the Africans who worked in the colonies were treated the same as the white servants who arrived from Europe. They had the same rights and could work for wages, save money, and start their own farms. By 1700, however, things had changed. White settlers began to regard all Africans as slaves. They gradually took away the rights of African settlers until most were slaves. The climate of the southern colonies made tobacco a lucrative crop, and more slaves were imported from Africa to work in the fields. Eventually, white colonists began to think of black men and women as different. They wrote new laws that treated whites and blacks differently, giving whites more rights and power over blacks. By the time the American Revolution began in the 1770s, most whites considered blacks to be inherently inferior to whites.

In the years after the Revolution, the number of slaves grew rapidly. The crops grown in the South, such as tobacco, corn, and cotton, were an essential part of the young country's economy, and plantation owners in the South needed more slaves to produce more crops. By the time Frederick was born, there were more than 2 million slaves in the United States. Most white Americans did not question whether slavery was right or wrong. It was just the way things were. To most of them, the promises of the Declaration of Independence and the Constitution did not apply equally to whites and blacks.

Frederick did not know the history of slavery when he arrived at the Lloyd plantation, but it did not take long for him to understand what it meant to be a slave. Nor did it take very long for him to begin questioning why he was a slave.

Fortunately for Frederick, Aaron Anthony's daughter, Lucretia Auld, took a liking to him. Sometimes she would

An 1881 engraving of a ship loaded with slaves

slip him an extra piece of bread and butter, and when Frederick was especially hungry, he would stand outside her window and sing, hoping for some food as a reward.

In 1826, when Frederick was eight years old, Lucretia and her husband, Thomas Auld, made a decision that changed Frederick's life forever. Aaron Anthony had become ill, so he and his family moved from the Lloyd plantation to a farm several miles away, taking some of their slaves with them. Thomas and Lucretia moved to a nearby town to run a small store. Instead of leaving Frederick behind to become a field hand on the Lloyd plantation, Thomas and Lucretia arranged to send Frederick to Baltimore to live with the family of Thomas's brother: Hugh Auld; Hugh's wife, Sophia; and their two-year-old son, Tommy. Frederick was leaving the plantation and heading to the city.

# Chapter 2

# An Educated Slave

Frederick had never felt at home on the plantation, so he was glad to leave. Even if things were not better, he thought, surely they could not be worse. On a Saturday morning, Frederick boarded a boat headed for Baltimore. Early the next morning, he arrived. A ship hand walked Frederick to his new home, where he was welcomed by the Aulds. The first thing Frederick noticed was the bright smile of Sophia Auld. It was the first time a white person had ever looked at him so kindly.

At the time, Baltimore was one of the largest cities in the United States, with more than 60,000 residents. Its crowded brick streets were quite a contrast to the quiet dirt roads of rural eastern Maryland. It was not easy for Frederick to get used to the bustle of life in Baltimore, and he sometimes found himself wishing he was back on the plantation. But for the first time in years, he also felt at home, mostly because of Sophia Auld. She gave him plenty to eat and new clothes to wear. She treated him almost as well as she treated her own son. Frederick now had a bed to sleep in and blankets to cover him. Hugh Auld did not show the same kindness as his wife, but he was not cruel, and Frederick was able to live without the constant fear of punishment that hung over him on the plantation. He also soon noticed that other slaves in Baltimore seemed better off than slaves on plantations.

It did not take long for Sophia Auld to realize that Frederick was a very bright young boy. She often read to him, usually from the Bible. When he asked her to teach him to read, she agreed. She began by going over the alphabet, and then she taught him to spell a few short words. Frederick learned quickly, impressing Sophia. Proud of her student, Sophia boasted to Hugh about Frederick's quick progress, expecting that he would be happy to find that Frederick could read.

An 1849 view of Baltimore Harbor from Federal Hill, with the Washington Monument in the background *(Courtesy of Maryland Historical Society)*

Instead, Hugh was furious. Most slaves were illiterate, and slave owners usually did their best to keep it that way. They feared that if slaves learned to read and write, it would put ideas in their head about freedom and make it easier for them to devise ways to escape. Sophia Auld had never had a slave in her house before, so she was not used to this kind of relationship. She hadn't understood that most slave owners would be outraged to find that she was actually teaching a slave to read. Hugh told his wife that teaching Frederick to read would ruin him for a life of hard labor. And, he added, it was both unsafe and illegal to teach a slave to read. It would make Frederick difficult to handle. "If you teach him how to read, he'll want to know how to write, and this accomplished, he'll be running away with himself," Hugh said.

Frederick listened as Hugh scolded his wife. He realized that if Hugh was so strongly opposed to teaching a slave to read, then reading must be important. He was now more determined than ever to continue his education, but he would have to do it on his own, without Sophia's help.

After Hugh's lecture, Sophia began to change in her attitude toward Frederick. She had treated him kindly at first, but now she began to learn how slave owners were supposed to treat their slaves. She would grow angry at him for the smallest offense, and she punished him when she caught him with the Bible or a newspaper trying to teach himself to read.

Now that he no longer had a teacher, Frederick began to resort to more devious tactics in his quest to read. When he went out to run an errand, he brought books with him. He finished his errands as quickly as possible and then sat for a few minutes by himself reading before returning to the house. He also enlisted the help of other boys he knew in the neighborhood.

He challenged them, declaring that he was sure that he could write as well as they could. When they took his challenge and wrote out a few words, Frederick quickly copied them down, adding to his growing vocabulary.

As time passed, Frederick's ability to read and write gradually improved. It helped once Tommy began school. Now Frederick could go through Tommy's old spelling workbooks and copy and recopy the words. When he couldn't find a spelling book, Frederick took down the Bible and copied passages over and over again. He always had to be careful: When Sophia caught him reading, she would rush over to him and furiously snatch away the book, warning him not to continue this behavior.

As Frederick grew older and continued his education, he repeatedly encountered one word in particular that gave him some trouble: *abolitionist*. He heard the word now and then, and it always seemed to have something to do with slavery. Sometimes he heard Hugh Auld use the word angrily, complaining about the actions of the abolitionists. Whenever there was a story of a slave hitting an overseer or killing a white person, Hugh would say that it was the fault of the abolitionists.

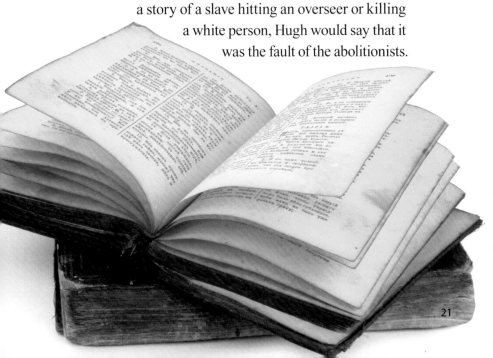

Hearing these stories made Frederick grow curious. But when he looked up the word *abolition* in the dictionary, it told him only that it was "the act of abolishing." That didn't help him much, because he didn't know what it was that was being abolished.

Later, Frederick came across a newspaper that had an article that used the word *abolition*. It said that Congress had received petitions from Northerners calling for the abolition of slavery in the District of Columbia. Frederick was excited. Not only had he learned the meaning of the word, but he now knew that there were actually people who wanted to abolish slavery. From then on, he always paid close attention when he heard or read anything to do with abolition.

Hugh Auld had been right in some ways. As Frederick improved his reading and writing, he began to think more and more about why he was a slave. "I wish I could be free," he said to some of his friends, young white boys about Frederick's age. "You will be free, you know," he told them. "But I am a slave for life. Have I not as good a right to be free as you have?" His friends always agreed with him that it was unfair, but Frederick had no idea what could be done.

One day, one of his young white friends read part of a speech from a book he had been assigned in school. The words intrigued Frederick, who decided that he wanted a copy of the book himself. He took fifty cents of the money he had carefully and slowly acquired over the years and went to a bookstore to buy this book, *The Columbian Orator*. It was a collection of speeches by famous men, from ancient Roman senators to American statesmen such as George Washington.

Although the book was not intended to support the abolition of slavery, many of the speeches were about the importance of liberty. One piece in particular struck Frederick. It was a fictional dialogue between a master and his slave in which the slave makes a strong argument against slavery—so strong that in the end the master agrees to free the slave. As Frederick read the dialogue, he imagined that one day he might speak well enough to earn his own freedom—if only he could learn to use words so powerfully and convincingly. He read the book over and over again, both increasing his limited vocabulary and making him hungrier to escape his fate as a slave.

As with learning the meaning of the word *abolition*, reading these speeches made Frederick hopeful. Perhaps he was not alone after all. There were others out there who agreed that slavery simply was not fair. He had sometimes wondered if there was a good reason for slavery—if perhaps God or nature had somehow intended that some people be slaves and others free. But after reading these speeches, Frederick never again questioned his right to be free. As he read, he grew angrier that anyone would prevent him from gaining that right. He thought to himself that slaveholders were no more than thieves; they had stolen the freedom of millions of men and women. He realized that Hugh Auld's prediction had come true. Now that Frederick could read, he would never again waver in his quest to become free.

Frederick's growing knowledge made his life with the Aulds more difficult. Sophia Auld no longer treated him as a son, and he no longer looked at her as a mother. Their relationship as master and slave ruined their friendship. Sophia now did what she could to prevent Frederick's growing independence, but Frederick was determined to thwart her efforts.

At the same time that Frederick was earnestly questioning the institution of slavery, other Americans, both black and white, were doing the same. On January 1, 1831, a white man in Boston named William Lloyd Garrison published the first issue of an abolitionist newspaper. Garrison would soon become the most famous abolitionist in the country—loved by the growing number of abolitionists in the North and hated by slave owners across the South. He filled his paper with accounts of the horrors of slavery and called for the immediate emancipation of all slaves.

That summer, thirteen-year-old Frederick heard the news of a slave rebellion in Virginia. A slave preacher named Nat Turner led a revolt, marching a small army of slaves from house to house killing white men, women, and children as they went. White militias ended the rebellion within two days, but not before Turner and his band had killed fifty-seven whites. The entire South became paralyzed. The fears of slave owners had come true. In the weeks following the revolt, whites killed more than

William Lloyd Garrison, publisher of the *Liberator* (Courtesy of the Library of Congress)

one hundred slaves on suspicion of being involved, although most had nothing to do with the rebellion. Turner himself was able to hide for two months before being caught and executed. When white Southerners talked about Nat Turner, they emphasized one point—he had learned to read. It was further evidence that it would only cause problems to educate slaves.

By now, of course, it was too late to quell Frederick's interest in education. Hugh Auld realized that the young slave was growing up quickly and that it would not be easy to keep him enslaved. Frederick was intelligent and stubborn, and he had no family ties binding him to the South.

So in March 1833, when Hugh Auld sent Frederick back to rural Maryland, he might have thought he was doing so for the young man's own good. Frederick was now fifteen, and Auld knew that if he tried to escape, it would mean either that Frederick would be lost forever to the North or possibly killed in the attempt.

Auld sent Frederick to live again with Thomas Auld, who had moved to the small town of St. Michaels. Aaron Anthony, Frederick's owner, had died in 1826, not long after Frederick first arrived in Baltimore. As part of Anthony's legal property, Frederick and Anthony's other slaves were divided up among Anthony's two children. Frederick had been allotted to Thomas and Lucretia Auld, who had allowed him to remain in Baltimore. When Lucretia died soon after, Frederick became the property of Thomas Auld.

Frederick had left the Lloyd plantation as a child. When he returned to live with Thomas Auld and his new wife, Frederick was fifteen, strong, stubborn, and convinced that he was not meant to live his life as a slave. That was a dangerous attitude for any slave. Slave owners did not like to have their authority questioned, and there was little tolerance of slaves who thought they were too good for slavery. Frederick worried as he sailed away from Baltimore toward St. Michaels. He knew that it would be much harder to run away from this small town than from the big city. At the same time, he resolved that somehow he would find a way to escape.

After living in the relative freedom of Baltimore, where he had been able to make friends and find time to himself, it was hard for Frederick to get used to life in rural Maryland again. His new mistress never seemed to give him enough food to eat, and the entire white community conspired to prevent slaves from learning to read and write. He spent his days working in the fields and his evenings trying to scrape together enough food to keep away hunger.

Frederick soon learned a new trick that helped him stay well fed. When his hunger got too great, he let Auld's horse get loose. For some reason, the horse always found its way to a

farm five miles away owned by Auld's father-in-law, William Hamilton. Mary, the slave who ran the kitchen at Hamilton's farm, always had something ready for Frederick to eat. "I never left there hungry," Frederick later recalled. Auld, however, didn't find Frederick's plan so amusing.

Soon Frederick was in more serious trouble. Despite the efforts of the white community, Frederick was able to find a way to spread the education he had received in Baltimore. A white man named Wilson asked Frederick to help him teach a Sunday school class for slaves at the house of a free black man. Wilson brought some old spelling books and Bibles to use to teach the slaves. About twenty students showed up for the first class. Frederick was overjoyed to be able to use what he had learned and to have a new purpose in his life. But the class did not last long. The next week, a mob of white men burst into the house and broke up the class. They warned Frederick never to attempt to start such a class again. One white man

told Frederick that if he kept up this behavior, he would end up like Nat Turner.

Thomas Auld continued to have trouble controlling his headstrong young slave. Before long, he was fed up with Frederick's attitude and worried that Frederick really might turn into the next Nat Turner. So in January 1834, less than a year after Frederick arrived from Baltimore, Auld sent Frederick to work for a white farmer named Edward Covey, who had a notorious reputation for being able to break slaves. Owners sent difficult slaves to Covey in the hope that he would break their spirit and make them easier to manage. In return for this service, Covey gained field hands for his small farm. Neither Frederick nor Covey had any idea what their year together would bring.

# Chapter 3
# Fighting to Survive

On New Year's Day, 1834, Frederick bundled up the little clothing he had and walked the seven miles to the farm where Edward Covey lived with his wife, his wife's sister, and a cousin. Frederick would not be the only slave. Covey owned one slave, a woman, and he hired several others.

It took only a few days for Frederick to learn that Covey's reputation for violence was well earned. Soon after Frederick arrived, Covey ordered him to take a cart and a team of oxen to pick up some wood stored about two miles from the house. Frederick was willing to do the work, but he had never learned how to drive oxen, and Covey made no offer to show him what to do.

Frederick hitched the oxen to the cart and began walking alongside them, leading them through an open field toward a path into the woods. The first mile or so through the field went smoothly, and the oxen seemed content to follow Frederick. But as the oxen approached the woods, something spooked them, and they suddenly began charging ahead at full speed. The cart started to rock back and forth, hitting trees and bouncing over stumps. Frederick ran behind trying to keep up. He worried that the oxen might get loose and that he might be crushed by the cart. Finally, after several minutes of this mayhem, the oxen crashed the cart into a tree and came to a stop.

Frederick was dazed. In the collision, the wheels had come off the cart and the oxen had become tangled in tree branches. After struggling to lift the heavy cart, Frederick eventually

managed to get the wheels back on. He then untangled the oxen and began leading them again to the wood pile.

Frederick loaded the wood onto the cart, adding an extra-heavy load in the hope that it would prevent the oxen from repeating their dash through the woods. By now half the day was spent, and Frederick worried that Covey would think he had been gone too long. When he finished, he took the oxen back toward the farm. When he came to the gate that led to the farm, Frederick let go of the rope to open the gate. As soon as the gate swung open, the oxen surged forward, crushing the gate with the cart—and nearly crushing Frederick as well.

After this close escape, Frederick and the oxen made their way back to the farm without any further trouble. Frederick told Covey what had happened. He thought Covey might

congratulate him for dealing with such a difficult team of oxen, but Covey said nothing at first. Then, he told Frederick to go back to the woods. As Frederick began retracing the route to the woods, he noticed that Covey was following him.

As soon as Frederick entered the woods, Covey told him to stop. Covey then cut three thin branches from a tree and trimmed them until they were narrow and supple—they made perfect whips. Covey ran at Frederick and began beating him with the switches until they were too broken to use. It was the worst beating Frederick had ever received, but it was only the beginning of many months of brutality at the hands of Covey.

Every week, Covey punished Frederick violently at least once, sometimes whipping him, other times beating him with sticks. The workdays began at dawn and did not end until the sun had set. Covey gave Frederick and the other slaves enough to eat but never enough time to eat the food they had. He would also sneak up on the slaves while they were in the fields to make sure they were working at full speed. He hid in the crops and then suddenly appeared out of nowhere. And whether it was hot or cold, sunny or snowy or rainy, Frederick and the other slaves were out in the fields working long days. Frederick and Bill Smith, another slave hired out to Covey, began calling Covey "the snake," because of his habit of slithering through the fields.

Between the constant beatings and the endless work, Frederick felt his spirit fading away. He no longer had the time or energy to worry about anything other than simply surviving to the next day. "Covey succeeded in breaking me," Frederick later wrote. "I was broken in body, soul, and spirit. My natural elasticity was crushed, my intellect languished."

Only on Sundays did Frederick have any time to himself. Even then, he was too tired to try to read. He often spent these valuable days lying under a tree, recovering from the previous week and preparing for the next week. From this spot he could look out at the Chesapeake Bay and watch the sailboats making their way through the waters. As he watched the boats, he could not help but feel sorry for himself. His hope for freedom slowly slipped away, and at times he even considered killing himself. Anything would be better than another week of this brutality, he thought.

Still, he managed to retain some hope that someday things would change. The boats on the bay reminded him of the possibility of making his way north to freedom. Then, in August, on one of the hottest days of the summer, Frederick's life took a new turn. Frederick, two other slaves, and Covey's cousin were working together to fan wheat—the process of separating wheat seeds from their cases. Frederick's job was to carry the wheat to the fan that separated the seeds. It was hard work, and by mid-afternoon Frederick started to feel dizzy. He tried to continue working, but suddenly he collapsed. He crawled into the shade to try to recover. Covey, who was standing nearby, saw that the work had stopped and went over to find out what had happened.

Bill Smith, another slave, told Covey that Frederick was sick and couldn't carry the wheat. Covey spotted Frederick lying in the shade and went over to him. He stood over Frederick and demanded to know what was wrong. Frederick tried to answer, but he couldn't speak. Covey kicked Frederick and began yelling at him to get up and get back to work. Frederick started to get up, but stumbled and fell back to the ground. Covey took a piece of wood and hit Frederick on the side of the head. After a few more kicks, Covey left Frederick lying on the ground with blood running from his head.

Frederick lay on the ground trying to recover his strength. He worried that he might bleed to death or be beaten further by Covey. When he saw Covey in the distance, Frederick climbed to his feet and began walking toward the woods. He decided he had to make it back to the Aulds before Covey killed him. To avoid being caught by Covey, he walked the entire seven miles in the woods, close enough to the road to find his way but hidden enough to avoid being spotted.

In his condition, it took Frederick five hours to make it the seven miles to the Aulds' farm. His hair and shirt were by now covered with blood, and his feet and legs were torn from walking through the thick brush. When Frederick told Auld what had happened, he expected Auld to be upset that his slave had nearly been killed. Instead, Auld told Frederick that it was undoubtedly his own fault. He must have done something wrong to upset Covey. Frederick asked to be sent somewhere else to work, but Auld refused. Auld told Frederick that he could spend the night there, but he would have to return to Covey's farm in the morning.

The next morning, a Saturday, Frederick set out for Covey's farm. By nine he was already there. As he approached the farm, he spotted Covey running toward him with a whip. Fearing for his life, Frederick ran into a cornfield, where the stalks of corn were so high that he was able to hide.

That night, Frederick hid at the home of Sandy Jenkins, a slave who worked on a nearby farm. Jenkins lived with his wife, a free black woman who had a cabin several miles from Covey's farm. On Sunday morning, Frederick again returned to Covey's farm, but this time he met a very different reception. Covey was on his way to church as Frederick arrived, and he said nothing to Frederick other than to ask him politely to do some work around the farm. Frederick began to wonder if perhaps Covey had changed his mind about whipping him.

On Monday, Frederick was ready to get back to work. Before the sun was even up, Covey asked Frederick to go feed the horses. Frederick went to the stables and started doing as Covey had asked. Covey then entered the stable with a rope and rushed at Frederick to catch him off guard. He grabbed Frederick's legs and began to tie him, trying to make sure that this time Frederick wouldn't get away. Without thinking, Frederick sprang to his feet, escaping Covey's grasp. Then, when Covey again approached Frederick, the young man grabbed Covey by the throat, holding him off. Covey likewise grabbed Frederick, and the two men stood there struggling to gain an advantage.

Covey was shocked. The punishment for a slave who struck a white man was often death, and just a few days earlier, Frederick had felt an intense fear of Covey. But as the fight continued, Frederick became more confident. Covey called to his cousin, who came to the stable to help Covey. But Frederick managed to kick Covey's cousin in the stomach even as he grappled with Covey, sending the cousin out of the fight. The battle went on for what seemed to Frederick like hours, with neither man able to gain an edge. Finally, tired and gasping for breath, Covey stopped fighting and declared that he had given Frederick enough of a beating for now. Frederick knew that he had won. He had stood up for himself and refused to let Covey whip him. For the rest of his time on Covey's farm, Frederick escaped without a single beating. Covey may have feared that if he tried again, Frederick might not let him off so easily. Frederick wondered why Covey did not report this rebellion and have him punished. But he realized that if Covey told others what had happened, it might ruin his reputation as a slave breaker. He could not let everyone know that a young teenager had managed to beat him.

On Christmas Day, Frederick's long year of labor under Covey finally ended. Like most slaves, Frederick had time to himself between Christmas and New Year's as a brief respite from hard work. He spent most of the time at St. Michaels before leaving again on New Year's Day to work for a man named William Freeland, who had hired Frederick for the next year. After months of agony, Frederick emerged from his year with Covey stronger than he had ever been and more convinced that he would not spend his entire life in slavery.

# Chapter
## 4
# Dreaming of Freedom

Frederick soon found that life working for William Freeland was quite different from his experience with Edward Covey. The workdays were still long, but Freeland gave slaves on his farm enough food to eat and enough time to eat it. He also rarely resorted to violence, which meant that Frederick could live without the constant threat of whipping hanging over his head. Even better for Frederick, he found good company in the fellow slaves working on Freeland's farm.

It did not take long for Frederick to become good friends with John and Henry Harris, two brothers who were owned by Freeland. Also working on the farm were two other hired slaves, Handy Caldwell and Sandy Jenkins, the man who had helped Frederick when he was hiding from Covey.

Thanks to these new friends, Frederick had a chance to put his reading and writing skills to work again. When they found out that Frederick could read, they asked him to teach them. John and Henry found some old spelling books, and Frederick agreed to lead a reading class on Sundays. Word soon spread to slaves on other farms that Frederick was teaching slaves to read, and others began showing up on Sundays to join the lessons. Eventually, more than forty slaves, both men and women, regularly attended the classes. They all knew that they had to keep quiet. If their masters found out, they would surely put the lessons to an end.

With the weeks spent working in the fields and Sundays spent teaching, the time passed quickly. As the year drew to a close, Frederick was glad to learn that Freeland intended to hire him again for the next year. He remembered how miserable life had been under Covey, and he had no desire to return to such conditions. At the same time, Frederick could not help feeling that time was slipping away. Another year had passed without getting any closer to his goal of escaping. He was happy to have found friends and to work for a master who refrained from violence, but he worried that the longer he waited, the harder it would be to escape. So as the new year approached, Frederick resolved that he would not let the next year pass without making an attempt to run away.

Frederick had dreamed of running away since he was a child, but it was still a difficult decision to make. His life working for William Freeland was better than it had been for a long time. If he were caught, he would most likely either be killed or sold to the Deep South.

Slaves in the Upper South (in states such as Maryland, Delaware, and Virginia) feared being sold to states farther south (such as Alabama, Georgia, and South Carolina).

As brutal as slavery was in the Upper South, it was thought to be even worse in the Deep South.

But for Frederick, the most painful part of contemplating escape was the thought of leaving behind his newfound friends. So he decided that perhaps they might want to try to escape with him. He started with the Harris brothers. He wanted to gauge their interest in running away without making them too suspicious. He quickly found that they were as excited about the idea as he was. Frederick then approached Sandy Jenkins and the two other slaves working at Freeland's farm. Soon their band was up to six, including Frederick. With the decision made to try to escape, Frederick began devising a plan.

It was not easy for a slave to make it from slavery to the free states of the North. For one thing, most slaves had little experience with geography. Frederick knew that the North meant freedom, but he had not even heard of many of the northern states, such as New York and Massachusetts. His knowledge did not extend any farther north than Pennsylvania and New Jersey.

Slave owners knew that by depriving slaves of an education, they made it that much harder for slaves to escape. Hugh Auld had said as much to Frederick when Frederick was young. But despite the many obstacles, thousands of slaves did eventually make their way to the North. There were a number of ways to try to escape, all of them difficult and risky.

Some slaves escaped with the help of an informal network of both blacks and whites who sheltered runaways and moved them north. This became known as the Underground Railroad. Free blacks in the South often gave runaways a place to stay until they could be sent north, where others helped them. Some slaves who escaped eventually became part of the Underground Railroad, helping other slaves to escape as well. Harriet Tubman, for example, who was born a slave in Maryland, escaped in 1849 and spent the next decade making secret trips back to the South to help others reach freedom.

Tens of thousands of slaves moved northward each year by way of the Underground Railroad, a network of people who helped fugitive slaves escape to the North and to Canada.

Other slaves escaped by coming up with their own plans. In 1849, a slave in Richmond, Virginia, named Henry Brown mailed himself to Philadelphia. With the help of a storekeeper in Richmond, Brown packed himself into a shipping crate, carrying some water with him. The storekeeper nailed the box shut and sent it on its way to Philadelphia, where a group of antislavery activists had agreed to pick it up. The box was marked to try to keep Brown's head up, but as soon as it arrived at the shipping office, the employees left it sitting upside-down. Brown spent the next twenty-seven hours bouncing around in the box on a ship, the railroad, and a wagon before finally arriving at his destination and emerging from the crate.

A more common technique was to escape by using a disguise. A husband and wife named William and Ellen Craft came up with their own ingenious plot. Ellen, whose skin was very light, cut her hair, dressed in men's clothes, and pretended to be a white slave owner heading north with a slave, who was her husband. Using this disguise, they made their way successfully to the North, where they soon began speaking about their experiences as slaves.

Living in Maryland, Frederick and his fellow slaves had the advantage of being close to the North. It was much more difficult for slaves from the Deep South states, such as Alabama and Georgia, to make it all the way to the North. Still, even though the free states loomed just north of Maryland, it would not be an easy trip.

The first difficulty was simply to get away from Freeland's farm undetected. Then, if they succeeded, they would have to escape the notice of the slave-catchers

Harriet Tubman made nineteen trips into the South and escorted more than three hundred slaves to freedom.
*(Courtesy of Library of Congress)*

who roamed the roads of the South looking for runaways. It would not be easy for six black men to go unnoticed. There were other factors as well. Even if they made it to the free states, they would face the constant threat of being returned to slavery. Under U.S. law, slave owners could reclaim escaped slaves in the North and bring them back to the South. Facing these odds, Sandy Jenkins decided that he would not take part in the escape after all. He might have worried that if he failed, he would never see his wife again.

The group was now down to five: Frederick; the Harris brothers; Frederick's uncle, Henry Bailey; and a slave named Charles Roberts, who was owned by Thomas Auld's father-in-law, William Hamilton. They decided to make their escape by water, and they planned to leave on the Saturday before Easter. It would be too difficult to travel unnoticed by road, so they would take a large canoe owned by William Hamilton and paddle up the Chesapeake Bay about seventy miles, sticking close to the shoreline to avoid the rough waters farther out in the Bay. Then they would return to land and follow the North Star by land to Pennsylvania. If they were spotted in the boat, they planned to act as fishermen. And in case they were stopped on land, Frederick wrote passes giving them permission to go to Baltimore for Easter, forging the signature of William Hamilton on each pass.

The last week before the attempt dragged on. Frederick noticed that his friends were growing more worried each day. He tried to reassure them, but he too was uneasy and wished the hours would go by more quickly. Finally, on Saturday morning, they went into the fields, planning to put their scheme into action later in the day. While working next to Sandy Jenkins, Frederick suddenly had a feeling of dread. They had been found out—he was sure of it.

At breakfast time, Frederick returned to the house and entered the kitchen. Through the window he saw four white men on horses at the front of the house. Behind them stood two black men, and it looked as if their hands were tied. William Hamilton rode up to the house and demanded to speak to Freeland. As they spoke, Freeland called Frederick to the door. The men seized Frederick and tied his hands together, and then they did the same to John Harris. Hamilton now told the men to search the slaves for any evidence, such as forged passes.

Frederick panicked—he realized that he had the forged pass in his pocket. If it were discovered, it would be hard evidence against him. But just as Freeland mentioned the passes, Henry Harris returned to the kitchen from the barn. Distracted from searching the slaves, the white men now approached Henry Harris and ordered him to put his arms together to be tied. "No, I won't!" Henry replied. The men pulled out their pistols and pointed them at Henry. Still he refused. "I won't be tied!" he declared. As he said it, he struck out at the men, knocking their guns to the ground. They all now jumped on him, finally tying him up. In the midst of commotion, with the white men distracted, Frederick took out his pass and dropped it into a fire used for cooking.

The white men now led Frederick and his fellow conspirators to the closest jail, fifteen miles away. With the search for the passes forgotten, Frederick whispered to the other slaves to eat their passes when they had a chance.

After Easter, Freeland and Hamilton arrived at the jail to take their slaves back with them. They blamed the plot on Frederick, thinking that the other slaves would not have had escape in their heads if not for him. Thomas Auld let Frederick sit in his cell for more than a week, perhaps deciding what to do with his troublesome slave. Slave traders passed by his cell, telling him they couldn't wait to get their hands on him to sell him farther south. Frederick worried that Auld would do exactly that, exiling him to the Deep South and cutting him off from any chance at escape.

Finally, Auld arrived at the jail and took Frederick back to St. Michaels, threatening to sell Frederick to slave owners in Alabama. He certainly could not keep Frederick around St. Michaels. Other slave owners in the area told Auld that Frederick was a troublemaker and that he would make it harder for them to manage their own slaves.

But instead of sending Frederick to a life of slavery in the Deep South, Auld decided to return him to Baltimore to live with Hugh and Sophia Auld. He told Frederick that he would learn a trade in Baltimore, and he promised to set Frederick free at the age of twenty-five—if he worked diligently in the meantime. Frederick did not really believe this offer, but he was surprised and happy to find that he would be returning to Baltimore. Once again, a decision to send Frederick to Baltimore changed his life forever.

When Frederick arrived in Baltimore for the second time, both he and the city had changed. He was no longer the little boy he had been when he first met Sophia and Hugh Auld. And Baltimore was now a large city of about 100,000. Over the years, the number of free black men and women in the city had also grown.

Hugh Auld soon got Frederick a job in a shipyard, where Frederick was to learn the trade of caulking while working as an apprentice. Caulkers applied waterproof materials, such as pine pitch, to the seams of ships to make the ships watertight. But when Frederick started working, the white men who worked as caulkers refused to work with a black man. Instead of learning a trade, Frederick was forced to do errands for the other workers. He spent his days running here and there. He would carry wood to one carpenter, only to have another man demand that he quickly bring him some tools. No matter how fast he moved, it was always too slow for the other workers.

Frederick took the verbal abuse of the other men, but he told himself that he would never allow himself to be beaten physically without putting up a fight. One white apprentice working at the shipyard soon found that out. He approached Frederick with a sharp tool, intending to put the young black man in his place. But Frederick fought back, holding off the man and refusing to give in.

It didn't take long for the white workers to realize that it would take more than one man to overpower Frederick. One day, a group of white apprentices surrounded him, hitting him with stones and bricks. When Frederick tried to fight back against the men in front of him, he felt a sharp blow from behind. He fell to the ground and the men jumped on, beating him nearly to death. Frederick lay on the ground trying to gain enough strength to get to his feet. With what little energy he had left, he began to get up. Just then, a man wearing heavy boots kicked Frederick in the eye, spilling blood everywhere. With that, the men left Frederick lying there bloodied and beaten.

After recovering for some time, Frederick finally got to his feet and stumbled home. Sophia Auld had done little to make Frederick feel welcome on his second stay with the family, but she could not help but take pity on him when she saw the extent of his wounds. She tended to him, wiping away the blood. Hugh was furious. He was determined to punish the men at the shipyard for what they had done. But when he went to the local magistrate to file a complaint, he was told that there was no evidence to punish anyone. None of the

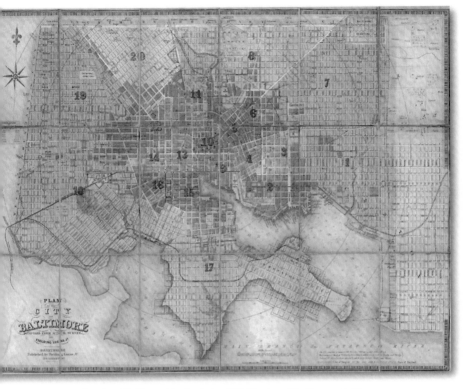

City plan of Baltimore, Maryland, circa 1852 *(Courtesy of Davidrumsey.com)*

white workers would testify against other white workers, and as a black man, Frederick was not allowed to testify against white men. Auld had to settle for finding Frederick a job at a different shipyard once Frederick was well enough to continue working.

Frederick appreciated the kindness shown to him by the Aulds after this attack, but the relationship between him and Hugh was growing increasingly strained. Nothing Hugh or Thomas Auld had done had succeeded in breaking Frederick's desire for independence, and now Hugh worried that the more freedom he gave Frederick, the more the young man would resist being a slave.

Since returning to Baltimore, Frederick had become closely involved in the free black community. He joined a club organized by a group of black men—the East Baltimore Mental Improvement Society—in which the men would meet to discuss politics and other issues. On occasion they even had formal debates. Once again, Frederick's intellectual curiosity was awakened, and he became more interested in improving his education. He also met a woman named Anna Murray, a free black woman living in Baltimore. The two began to spend time together, and before long they had grown close. Frederick enjoyed having these friends to fill the hours he had free from work, but seeing them was also a constant reminder that he remained a slave.

When Frederick went back to work, he did so this time as a caulker. He was soon making quite a bit of money for Auld. Frederick earned $1.50 a day for his work, so some weeks he would bring home as much as $9 to Auld. He resented having to give his earnings to Auld. He had done the work; why didn't he deserve to keep the money? Frederick saw no reason that Auld had a right to the money he had worked hard to earn.

When Frederick brought him his earnings at the end of each week, Auld would look at him and ask, "Is this all?" Some weeks, as an encouragement, he gave Frederick six cents out of the $6 or so that Frederick earned. Auld thought he was being generous to give Frederick anything. After all, Frederick was a slave, and Auld was his master. He had the legal right to all of the money. But Frederick never accepted that reasoning. When Auld gave him a few cents, it only made Frederick angrier that he did not get to keep all of it.

When Thomas Auld visited Baltimore in the spring of 1838, Frederick took the chance to make a deal with him. Frederick said that if Auld allowed him to hire himself out without constant oversight, he would pay for his own room and board and still give Hugh Auld most of what he earned every week. In return, Frederick would get more freedom over his time and the opportunity to save the extra money he made—perhaps even enough money to buy his freedom. This was a common situation among skilled slave workers. It allowed owners to have constant income without having to monitor their slave so closely.

But Thomas Auld was not happy with Frederick's proposal. He knew that Frederick was a headstrong and independent young man, and he worried that if he gave Frederick any more freedom than he already had, it would only be a matter of time before he tried again to escape. He assured Frederick that he would take care of him, that there was no need to try to earn enough money to buy his own freedom.

Frederick was disappointed, but he did not give up. Two months later, in May, he made the same proposal again, this time to Hugh Auld. Frederick did not realize that Thomas and Hugh had discussed the matter. Hugh was surprised that Frederick would be so bold as to ask again when he had already been refused once. But after thinking it over, Hugh agreed to Frederick's plan. Frederick would have to find his own place to live, pay for his own food, and buy his own tools for work. At the end of every week, Frederick would have to give $3 to Auld, regardless of whether he had been able to find work that week. Frederick knew that he would have to work hard just to make enough to pay for his room and board and the $3 he owed Auld every week. But he was determined to make it work. He thought this could be a step toward freedom; eventually, he might be able to save enough money to buy his freedom or escape to the North.

Autographed portrait of Frederick
Douglass, by engraver John
Chester Buttre *(Courtesy of North
Wind Picture Archives/Alamy)*

Engraved by J.C.Buttre.

For the next several months, Frederick fulfilled his end of the deal, sometimes working odd jobs both day and night to make enough to give Auld his $3. When he wasn't working, he spent time with Anna Murray and with other black men and women living in Baltimore. He was more at home than he had been at any time since working with his friends on William Freeland's farm. But just as Frederick had been restless then, worrying that he might never be free, he began to worry again that he would spend his entire life in slavery.

Frederick's hatred of slavery made him resent having to report to Auld every week. The more freedom Frederick had, the more he wondered why he should not be completely free. In August, his growing confidence almost made him lose the little freedom he had gained.

Every Saturday after work, Frederick was required to deliver his $3 to Hugh Auld. One Saturday, Frederick made plans with some friends to attend a religious camp meeting outside Baltimore after he finished work. These were popular social gatherings, and Frederick was excited to go. When his work took longer than he had planned, he had to decide whether to stop at the Aulds' house, which would mean missing his friends for their trip to the camp meeting, or to go to the meeting without first giving Auld the $3. Frederick decided that it would not be a problem to give Auld the money the next day, so he met up with his friends and left Baltimore for the gathering.

Once there, Frederick was enjoying himself too much to get away on Sunday, and he ended up staying at the meeting until Monday. On Monday morning, Frederick left early and went straight to see Hugh Auld with his $3. Auld was furious. He had feared that Frederick had run away. He demanded to know why Frederick had not appeared on Saturday and what made Frederick think that he could choose not to show up. "I have a great mind to give you a severe whipping," Auld told him. Frederick, who had not been whipped in years, was infuriated by Auld's reaction. He felt that he had earned the right to be trusted—and the right to control his time. Auld finally concluded the argument by telling Frederick that their arrangement was finished. From now on, Frederick would live with the Aulds as before.

Frederick obeyed, bringing his tools and other belongings to the Aulds. That week, however, he did not earn a single dollar. He left the house in the morning and returned in the evening, but he did not try to find any work. On Saturday, Auld demanded his $3. Frederick replied that he had not earned any money. Auld was astounded by Frederick's actions. The argument between the two men grew fierce, and it even seemed that it might result in a fight. Fortunately for Frederick, Auld simply resolved to find work for Frederick. Once Frederick calmed down, he realized that if he continued to anger Auld, it might only be a matter of time before he was sent back to St. Michaels, or perhaps even sold to the Deep South. He made up his mind that it would be better to remain in Baltimore, and to make another attempt to flee slavery. With his mind made up, he set early September as the date of his escape.

# Chapter
# 5
# Northward Bound

The next Monday, Frederick woke up early, left the house, and found work on his own. He wanted to put Auld's mind at rest. By the end of the week, he had more than eight dollars to hand over to his master. Frederick's agreeableness eased the tensions between the two men. Auld again began to trust Frederick to do his work and return with his pay. Meanwhile, Frederick continued to plan his escape.

This time, Frederick had to succeed. There was little chance that the Aulds would allow him to remain in Baltimore if he was caught, and the other slave owners in St. Michaels had already had enough of his trouble-making. He would be leaving behind all of his friends in the Baltimore community. If he failed, he would probably never see Anna Murray again.

Planning the escape was not easy. Whites knew it would be tempting for slaves just to get on a train headed north, so they made it as difficult as possible for a slave to take the train without being caught. Free blacks had to carry papers that proved that they were free, and blacks could be stopped at any time and asked for their papers. Even free blacks were only allowed to travel during the day. Boats were also under constant surveillance. Frederick did not have free papers, of course. But he did have a friend, a free black man, who resembled Frederick. The man, who worked as a sailor, agreed to lend Frederick his sailor's papers, which proved that the sailor was a free man. The papers had an emblem with an eagle and a description of the free man.

Frederick planned to leave on Monday, September 3. The week before he left, he worked as always, but he worried that something would go wrong. Frederick had spent most of his Sundays away from the Aulds' house. Not wanting to raise any suspicions, he did the same on September 2, although he had nowhere in particular to go. The next morning, he woke up early, left the house, and never returned.

A carriage driver named Isaac Rolls had arranged to pick Frederick up and take him to the train station. They planned to arrive just before the train left. That way, Frederick could buy his ticket when he was already on board the train. If he tried to buy the ticket at the station, the papers would likely be closely examined. The resemblance to the sailor was close, but Frederick's skin was lighter than his friend's. If anyone read the papers carefully, they would surely realize that Frederick was not the owner of the papers. To keep up the disguise, Frederick dressed like a sailor, with a red shirt and a black cravat—a piece of cloth tied loosely around his neck.

Isaac pulled into the station with Frederick right on time. Frederick boarded the train and found a seat in the cabin reserved for black passengers. The train was already out of Baltimore by the time the conductor made his way into Frederick's compartment. As the conductor approached, Frederick grew tense, but he tried to appear calm.

"I suppose you have your free papers," the conductor said to Frederick.

"No, sir. I never carry my free papers to sea with me," Frederick replied.

"But you have something to show that you are a free man, have you not?"

"Yes, sir," Frederick said. "I have a paper with the American eagle on it that will carry me round the world."

Frederick showed the conductor his papers, but the conductor merely glanced at them before moving on. He had passed the first test, but he was still far from safety.

The time dragged by as Frederick waited for the train to make its way north. It crossed into Delaware, also a slave state, and arrived at the Susquehanna River. There the train stopped, and the passengers boarded a ferry to cross to the other side, where they would take another train to continue their trip. On the ferry, a black man from Baltimore recognized Frederick and began talking to him, asking him where he was going. Frederick tried to avoid the conversation, and he slipped away as soon as he had a chance.

That was not the only close call. On the next train, Frederick realized that a white blacksmith he knew was taking the same train. The man stared at Frederick as if he recognized him, and Frederick feared that his escape had failed. But the man said nothing, and Frederick's journey continued.

The last change came in Wilmington, Delaware, where Frederick took a steamboat headed for Philadelphia. That afternoon, the ship reached the city. He then took another train, this time to New York City, arriving there the next morning. Frederick Bailey had finally escaped. "It was a moment of the

Aerial view of New York City
*(Courtesy of Photo Art Collection (PAC)/Alamy)*

highest excitement I ever experienced," he later wrote. "I felt like one who had escaped a den of hungry lions."

Frederick Bailey was hungry, tired, and lonely, but for the first time in his life, he was a free man. He knew, however, that the streets of New York City might not be a safe place for

a recently escaped slave. He stayed on the lookout for anyone who glanced at him curiously, worrying that they might be a slave-catcher. Through friends in Baltimore, he had made plans to meet up with a man named David Ruggles, who was part of a network of New Yorkers who helped runaway slaves when they arrived in the city. But Frederick did not know how to find where Ruggles lived, and he was too afraid of being caught to ask for help.

Within just a few hours of wandering the streets, Frederick spied a man named Jake whom Frederick had known in Baltimore. Jake had also been a slave, until, like Frederick, he escaped to New York. Frederick was happy to see a familiar face, but Jake soon made his worries even worse. Jake, who now called himself William Dixon, said that his owners had almost captured him soon after his escape, and that it was not safe to trust anyone. Even other black men could not be trusted, Jake warned, because some of them had been paid by white slave-catchers to betray runaway slaves. Jake looked nervous even while talking to Frederick, and he soon hastened away, seemingly afraid that even Frederick might be part of a plot to capture him.

Now Frederick was even more worried than before. He walked the streets of the city on the lookout for anyone suspicious. For two days he wandered without knowing where he was going, sleeping wherever he could find a place to hide. Finally, just when Frederick felt hopeless, he had a stroke of good luck. He noticed a black man looking at him, and he decided that he would take a chance and ask for help. The man turned out to be a sailor named Stuart, and he helped Frederick find the house of David Ruggles.

Once with Ruggles, Frederick felt relieved. To help him escape attention should the Aulds try to capture him, Frederick decided to change his last name to Johnson. While staying with Ruggles, Frederick wrote a letter to Anna Murray, who was waiting anxiously behind in Baltimore, to let her know that he had made it safely. They had planned to meet once Frederick escaped, and so she followed him to New York. Within weeks of Frederick's escape from slavery, he and Anna were married.

Ruggles helped Frederick and Anna plan their next step. Frederick told Ruggles that he was a caulker, so Ruggles suggested that they move to New Bedford, Massachusetts, a busy shipbuilding port. Anna and Frederick boarded a steamship for Newport, Rhode Island, where they would take a carriage to New Bedford. There they went to the home of Nathan and Mary Johnson, who were friends with Ruggles and who would help Frederick and Anna get established in their new home.

One of the first problems Frederick dealt with upon arriving in New Bedford was his name. He found that his new town was full of people with the last name Johnson, including his host. He chose to change it to Douglass on a suggestion from Nathan Johnson. Before long, there was another Douglass— Anna gave birth to a daughter, Rosetta, not long after moving to New Bedford. The next year, Anna and Frederick had their first son, Lewis.

Growing up in the South, Frederick had learned very little about what life was like in the North. He had expected to find widespread poverty because there were no slaves to perform all the labor. Instead, he found well-kept houses, beautiful churches, blooming gardens, and more wealth than he could have imagined. "The people looked more able, stronger, healthier, and happier, than those of Maryland," he wrote. "But the most astonishing as well as the most interesting thing to me was the condition of the colored people, a great many of whom, like myself, had escaped" from slavery to the North. Douglass even came across a number of black men and women who had escaped from slavery within the past decade yet who already seemed to have finer houses and more wealth than the average slaveholder he knew in Maryland.

Douglass was shocked when Johnson told him that in Massachusetts it was even legal for a black man to hold public office. Johnson also reassured him that, at least in New Bedford, it was unlikely for an escaped slave to be returned to slavery, because there were many white residents who strongly disagreed with slavery and would defend runaway slaves against slave-catchers.

Nathan Johnson was a good example of the success of some blacks in the North. Douglass noticed that his house was full of books and that Johnson read newspapers and was able to speak more intelligently about politics and other topics than most slaveholders.

Douglass was encouraged by these observations, and he excitedly set out to find work, hoping to become as successful as those he saw around him. On his first afternoon in New Bedford, Douglass walked to the wharves and watched the busy shipbuilders at work. His first money earned as a free man came from shoveling coal in the cellar of a local minister, for which he earned $1. On his third day, Douglass found work helping to load cargo. The work was hard and dirty, but Frederick was happy to be working. He was excited to earn wages and not have anyone take those earnings away from him.

The next day, Douglass began looking for a job as a caulker. He found an employer almost immediately, but the white workers declared that they would go on strike if a black man was employed as a caulker. They did not want more competition for the skilled trades. With this obstacle, Douglass set out to make a living doing manual labor. He spent his days shoveling coal, sawing wood, cleaning chimneys—anything he could find to make a living. The pay was only half of what he would have been paid as a caulker, but Douglass still enjoyed the feeling of earning and keeping his own money.

Douglass found, as many other blacks in the North already knew, that racism was not something

A 1903 etching by Lemuel D. Eldred of ships and boats in the New Bedford Harbor *(Courtesy of the Library of Congress)*

confined to the South. At the time he arrived in the North, only four states—Vermont, Maine, Massachusetts, and New Hampshire—allowed black men to vote. Other laws in some northern states prevented blacks from serving on juries or testifying in court against whites.

Before long, Douglass found more consistent work in an oil refinery, moving and lifting large barrels of oil. There he met three other young black men, all of whom struck him as thoughtful and intelligent. He then began working in a brass foundry. He was young and strong, and there was much manual labor to be done. But it would not be long before it was Douglass's intellect rather than his brawn that earned him a living.

The first winter in New Bedford was hard. Prices for food were high, and despite his hard work, Douglass did not make a lot of money. He and Anna rented two rooms, and he managed to make enough to rent the rooms and buy enough food to get by.

About four months after moving to New Bedford, a man asked Douglass if he wanted to buy a subscription to a weekly paper called the *Liberator*. Douglass did not have the money to buy this luxury, but after he told the young salesman that he had just escaped from slavery and did not have the money to pay for a subscription, the salesman told him he would add him as a subscriber anyway. When Douglass began reading the paper, he was deeply impressed. The *Liberator* was published by an abolitionist in Boston named William Lloyd Garrison. Garrison was perhaps the nation's most famous abolitionist. He had started publishing his paper in 1831, and he used it to denounce slavery and to call for immediate emancipation of the slaves. The paper had caused quite a stir over the years, and many southern politicians had called for the governor of Massachusetts to prevent Garrison from publishing it.

Douglass began to look forward to the paper's arrival and devoured its contents. He admired the way Garrison spoke out boldly against slavery. Thus, Douglass was excited when he heard that Garrison was going to come to New Bedford in the spring of 1839 to give a speech. Frederick decided to see this man in person. When the day arrived, Douglass sat and listened to Garrison lecture about the evils of slavery. He was as impressed by Garrison's speaking as he was by his writing. This experience sparked Douglass's interest in becoming part of this antislavery movement. He wondered if he had something that he could contribute to the effort to end slavery. He began attending antislavery meetings held in New Bedford and talking to friends about the abolitionist movement.

In 1841, three years after making his escape from slavery, Douglass embarked on a new career. In August, he traveled to the island of Nantucket, off the coast of Massachusetts, to attend an antislavery convention held by the Massachusetts Anti-Slavery Society (MAS), which had been created by Garrison and other abolitionists in 1831. Douglass had been encouraged to attend by a Quaker businessman named William Coffin, who had heard Douglass talking about abolitionism at small meetings of black residents in New Bedford.

When Douglass arrived at the convention, Coffin found him and mentioned that he should try to speak at the meeting. A number of other speakers went to the front of the hall to discuss their views on slavery, and as the evening passed, Douglass tried to work up the courage to speak himself. Finally, near the end of the night, he stood up and asked to talk. He

Frederick Douglass, circa 1844

began by describing his life as a slave, and then he said that he had only within the last few years escaped to the North. Although Douglass was nervous, the crowd of more than one thousand listened quietly and attentively, struck by the words of this former slave.

After Douglass finished, Garrison stood up. He asked those in the crowd whether they would ever allow a man such as Frederick Douglass to be returned to slavery in the South.

"No!" the crowd shouted.

"Will you succor and protect him as a fellow man?" Garrison then asked.

"Yes," the listeners responded.

The night soon ended, but Douglass's new career was just beginning. After the speech, a man named John Collins, who worked for the Massachusetts Anti-Slavery Society, asked Douglass if he would like to start working for the MAS as a lecturer, traveling around the North giving speeches about his experiences as a slave. Douglass answered that he hardly felt qualified for such a task, but Collins, Garrison, and others eventually convinced him to join the abolitionist movement full-time. Douglass consented at first only to a three-month trial period, hesitant as he was about his abilities to succeed.

# Chapter
# 6
# A New Career

It was an exciting time for Douglass to begin his career as an abolitionist. It had been ten years since Garrison had gotten the movement going with the publication of his paper and the organization of the Massachusetts Anti-Slavery Society. Over those ten years, hundreds of other small anti-slavery organizations had sprung up across the North. The movement was still small, and most white Americans in both the South and North supported slavery, but it was growing. Garrison often drew hundreds of listeners to his speeches, although he occasionally drew angry crowds as well.

There was much work to be done in both the North and South. The North benefited economically from slavery just as the South did. Cotton grown in the South was brought to textile mills in the North and turned into finished products, such as clothes, that were then sold. Racism was deeply entrenched in northern society, as Douglass had discovered when he tried to get work as a caulker. Occasionally, abolitionist meetings would end in violence, as proslavery Northerners would interrupt the proceedings. In 1837 in Alton, Illinois, an abolitionist editor named Elijah Lovejoy was killed by a proslavery mob.

The federal government was no supporter of abolitionism. Most politicians, from both the North and South, supported slavery and opposed abolitionist rhetoric. They saw the abolitionists as a distraction. Throughout the 1830s, abolitionists led efforts to gather thousands of signatures on petitions against slavery. In 1836, petitions with more than 30,000 signatures were sent to Congress, which eventually became so fed up with these efforts that it enacted a "gag rule." It would no longer allow any discussion of these antislavery petitions.

But despite this opposition, the movement continued to grow. By 1840, in fact, it had grown large enough that it had split into two groups that disagreed about the best way to go about ending slavery. On one side of this debate were the Garrisonians—the abolitionists who sided with William Lloyd Garrison. Garrison believed that abolitionists should avoid politics. He thought that if abolitionists tried to end slavery by going through the political process—such as by supporting candidates for office—it would inevitably result in forcing the abolitionists to compromise their beliefs. He believed in continuing to write and speak about slavery as a moral issue. He felt that slavery was wrong, and he hoped eventually to convince enough white Americans that he was right that slavery should be ended. He believed that if the South would not give up slavery, then the northern states should break apart the Union by creating a separate country. "No union with slave-holders," was his oft-repeated motto.

On the other side of the issue were the political abolitionists. These abolitionists also believed that slavery was immoral, but they thought that the best way to end slavery was to try to use the political process to their advantage by, for example, running candidates for office.

In 1840, the disagreements between these two sides resulted in a split of the movement. At the annual convention of the American Anti-Slavery Society (AAS), many of the political abolitionists walked out in protest of Garrison's control of the society and formed their own antislavery group, which they called the American and Foreign Anti-Slavery Society. That fall, they even ran a candidate for president, a wealthy New Yorker named Gerrit Smith. Smith won very few votes, about 7,000, but the effort still marked a new kind of abolitionism.

At this point, Douglass was very much a Garrisonian. He was in awe of Garrison's speaking ability, and he agreed that slavery was a moral issue that had to be addressed by changing people's views of slavery. Douglass had found a strong role model in Garrison. Since he had first come across the *Columbian Orator* as a child, Douglass had always deeply respected the ability of words to change people's lives and attitudes. Now it was his turn to use words to try to change the course of history.

Garrison and others believed that if white Northerners could see someone like Douglass—someone who had lived through slavery firsthand—they might be less willing to support the institution. Douglass did not have any formal education, and he had not yet read as widely as some other

abolitionist speakers, but he knew what it meant to be a slave, and he had the ability to tell his story and to convince listeners to sympathize with him.

After agreeing to start working for the AAS, Douglass traveled around New England, mostly in Massachusetts, with George Foster, another AAS speaker. Even traveling was not always easy. Railroad cars were often segregated, with separate cars set aside for black passengers. On one trip to Dover, New Hampshire, Douglass refused to sit in the "Negro car" when told to move from the "white car" by the conductor. With the help of several other white men, the conductor eventually threw Douglass out of the car.

For the first few months, Douglass spoke almost solely about his life as a slave. He described his experiences, recounted the times he had seen slaves whipped or even killed, and repeated stories of the daily cruelties of slave owners. But Douglass also talked about prejudice in the North. "Prejudice against color is stronger north than south; it hangs around my neck like a heavy weight," he said in one speech in Lynn, Massachusetts, in October 1841.

As he read more about abolitionism, Douglass could not help but want to speak on issues other than his own experiences as a slave. He knew that it was important to remind his audiences of his firsthand experiences, but he also had developed strong intellectual and moral arguments against slavery, and he became bored with simply repeating the story of his slave life over and over again. His fellow abolitionists encouraged Douglass to stick to the story of his life rather than engage in more intellectual arguments. "Give us the facts, we will take care of the philosophy," John Collins told him. Collins and others knew that if Douglass spoke too eloquently against slavery, white audiences would stop believing that he had actually ever been a slave. They assumed that no slave could ever learn to speak to well. "People won't believe you were ever a slave, Frederick, if you keep on this way," Foster told him.

In fact, that is exactly what happened. Audiences no longer believed that this eloquent man could have been a slave. Part of the problem was that Douglass did not give the details of his enslavement in his speeches. He did not mention his master's name or the town or state where he had lived out of fear that Thomas Auld would hear about his work and come north to claim him as an escaped slave. Even with these precautions, some of Douglass's black friends told him that he was foolish for becoming a public figure. Douglass was in quite a bind. If he revealed the details of his life as a slave, he risked losing his freedom. But if he did not, he risked losing his credibility with audiences.

For the time, at least, Douglass chose to keep those details unexplained, but he remained busy traveling around the North. In 1843, he and other members of the AAS embarked on an effort to hold one hundred antislavery meetings in New England, New York, Ohio, Pennsylvania, and Indiana. Douglass would be expanding his speaking territory to the west.

The states to the west of New York were difficult territory for the abolitionists. These states bordered slave states, and as in New England and New York, many whites in these states sympathized with the slaveholders and angrily opposed the abolitionists. At Douglass's first meeting, in Richmond, Indiana, proslavery whites broke up the meeting and threw eggs at the speakers.

The next meeting, in Pendleton, Indiana, went even worse. None of the owners of the buildings in town would allow the abolitionists to speak. Douglass was now traveling with a white man, George Bradburn, and a black man, William White. The men set up a speaking platform and seats in the woods on the edge of town. More than one hundred men and women gathered to hear the speeches. As Bradburn began to speak, Douglass noticed that there were a number of men in the crowd who seemed threatening. At one point, the leaders of this gang ordered the abolitionists to stop speaking. White and Bradburn attempted to discuss the matter with the leaders of the mob, but the mob rushed at them and began beating them. Douglass tried to pick up a stick to defend himself, making the mob even angrier. They overwhelmed him, throwing him to the ground and beating him until he was unconscious. As Douglass lay on the ground, White grabbed a piece of wood being swung at Douglass, deflecting the blow. Fortunately, all three survived, and they soon continued their tour.

In 1844, Douglass decided to try to put an end to the speculation that he had never actually been a slave. He began writing an account of his life in slavery that would include details about his owner and his upbringing. His friends in the abolitionist movement, including Wendell Phillips, encouraged him in this effort. He continued to travel and speak while working on the book, and it was finally published in June 1845. *Narrative of the Life of Frederick Douglass, An American Slave, Written by Himself* was soon available for the price of fifty cents. Readers in the North proved eager to hear

Wendell Phillips *(Courtesy of the Library of Congress)*

Douglass's story, and more than 30,000 copies were sold over the next five years.

Now that Douglass had told his story, he knew it was no longer necessary to hide the details of his slavery. On May 6, 1845, he spoke at the annual meeting of the AAS and gave a preview of his forthcoming book. In his speech, Douglass announced

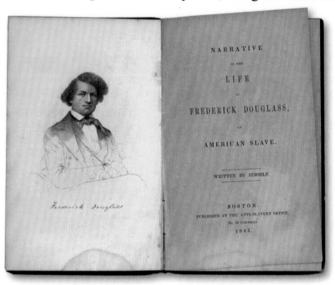

Douglass's autobiography *(Courtesy of the National Park Service)*

that he had lived on a plantation owned by Colonel Edward Lloyd in eastern Maryland. Douglass said that he knew that revealing this information could prove costly and even result in being returned to slavery, but he thought that the risk was worth being able to prove that he had been a slave. Douglass listed the names of overseers who had whipped slaves, and he told the story of the murder of the slave Denby by the overseer Austin Gore. This speech would be one of the last public appearances Douglass would make in the United States for two years.

As with Douglass's speeches, the clear and powerful writing in his autobiography raised suspicions among some that a former slave could not possibly write so well. But both Garrison and Phillips wrote introductions that were included with the book, and Douglass even included "Written by Himself" in the title to try to convince the public that he was, indeed, the author.

With every copy sold, the risk that Auld would try to recapture Douglass grew. Under federal law, Auld had the right to seize Douglass and return him to slavery. So with the encouragement of Garrison, Phillips, and other friends, Douglass decided to cross the Atlantic and spend time in England, Ireland, and Scotland. The British had long held slaves on West Indian islands but had abolished slavery in 1833. Since then, British abolitionists had remained active in the fight for abolition in the United States. Douglass's narrative had already been published in Europe and been well received. Now the author himself would make an appearance.

The months Frederick Douglass spent in Great Britain gave him a view of what life could be like if the color of his skin did not determine the way he was judged. Douglass could not get his own cabin onboard the *Cambria*, the ship that brought him across the Atlantic, because of his color, but other than that he found his fellow travelers quite welcoming. He traveled with James Buffum, a white abolitionist from Lynn, Massachusetts. Most of the trip went quietly enough, but on the last night at sea, the captain invited Douglass to give a speech. As Douglass spoke against slavery and the slave trade, two passengers began loudly interrupting him. Some of the passengers from southern states were insulted by Douglass's lecture and even threatened to throw him overboard. The captain put an end to the dispute by threatening to lock the two men in irons, which quickly quieted them.

The ship arrived without further incident in Liverpool, England. After a day spent in that port city, Douglass and

St. George's Hall, Liverpool, England, circa 1890s
*(Courtesy of the Library of Congress)*

Buffum traveled to Ireland, where they spent several weeks and stayed with families sympathetic to the American abolitionist movement.

As Douglass traveled out of the country for the first time, he reflected on what the United States meant to him. He wrote in a letter to Garrison, "In thinking of America, I sometimes find myself admiring her bright blue sky, her grand old woods, her fertile fields, her beautiful rivers, her mighty lakes, and star-crowned mountains." But he also thought of slavery. "America will not allow her children to love her," he wrote. Douglass felt conflicted about his homeland. On the one hand, he loved the geography and he had made friends and found help as a runaway slave. On the other hand, he was disgusted that the country would maintain slavery and prevent so many people from being free simply because of the color of their skin. He felt patriotism toward his country, but he also felt rejected by it. "The land of my birth welcomes me to her shores only as a slave," he wrote.

On one of his first days in Dublin, Douglass met with publisher Richard Webb, who planned to publish Douglass's narrative in Great Britain. Douglass gave a number of speeches, often hosted in Irish churches. He criticized the United States for slavery, and he criticized churches in Ireland and England that did not protest strongly enough against the slaveholding practices of their American counterparts.

On October 1, 1845, Douglass gave one of his first speeches in a foreign country, in a music hall that held approximately 3,000 people. "I am the representative of three millions of bleeding slaves. I have felt the lash myself; my back is scarred with it," Douglass said. One newspaper account of this speech said of Douglass, "He is a speaker of great ability, well calculated to interest the feelings and convince the judgment of his hearers."

Douglass also read excerpts from various laws in the slave states that showed the brutality of slavery. Douglass made quite an impact on his listeners. He was introduced by the mayor of Cork for a speech given on October 14. In that speech, he reminded his listeners that in the U.S. he was still considered a slave. Many of his speeches would last for hours, as Douglass would recount his time as a slave and denounce the perpetuation of slavery. He would also read advertisements printed in southern newspapers in which slave owners described runaway slaves in an attempt to get them returned.

One, for example, read:

> **Ran away a negro woman and two children—a few days before she went off, I burned her with a hot iron the left side of her face.**

Another read:

> **Ran away, Anthony; one of his ears cut off, and his left hand cut with an axe.**

From Cork, Douglass traveled to Limerick and then to Belfast, where he spent Christmas and spoke several times. In the new year, Douglass set out for Scotland. He traveled first to Glasgow and then on to Aberdeen, Perth, Edinburgh, and other Scottish cities. He proved to be a big draw, with large crowds of Scots attending his speeches. There were some listeners who did not approve of his fiery rhetoric, thinking that it might be better to appeal to southern Presbyterians to treat their slaves well, if they would not free them. But Douglass was not one for compromise. As in Ireland, Douglass caused quite a stir with his appearances and attracted thousands to his speeches.

By May, Douglass was in London, where he met up with William Lloyd Garrison. He and Garrison spent time with a number of prominent English abolitionists. While visiting the town of Newcastle, he met a woman named Ellen Richardson, who ran a girls school. He talked to her about returning to the United States and the danger he faced of being returned to slavery.

Richardson was moved by his story, and she decided that she would try to raise enough money to buy his freedom.

Before Douglass left to return to the U.S., she had raised money for this purpose and contacted Thomas Auld through a lawyer. The two sides agreed upon the price of $1,250. On November 30, 1846, Thomas Auld accepted the money, and on December 12, 1846, Hugh Auld filed the paperwork that freed Frederick Bailey. He was no longer a slave in the eyes of the American government.

Some abolitionists criticized Douglass for accepting this purchase, saying that he should have refused to allow any money to be used to purchase him. But Douglass, and many of his friends, believed that it was better to remove the risk that he would be returned to slavery.

As he traveled around Great Britain, Douglass could not help but contrast the warm welcome he received with the treatment he had often experienced in the United States. He had been thrown out of railroad cars and denied seats at taverns at home. But in Great Britain, he found himself able to travel freely without feeling any mark of different treatment because of his race.

Douglass enjoyed his time abroad so much that he even considered moving his family to England. He and Anna now had four children. Frederick Douglass, Jr., was born in 1842, and Charles Remond Douglass was born in 1844. Before much longer, he and Anna added their fifth and final child, Annie, to their family. Douglass wondered what it would be like to raise a family without worrying that his children's skin color would hinder their success. Finally, however, he decided that he could not abandon the fight against slavery, and he returned to the United States as planned in 1847.

# Chapter 7

# Tactical Decisions

Douglass had been acclaimed as a celebrity while in Great Britain, but it did not take long for him to find that in the United States he was still not considered the equal of white men and women. He had paid for a cabin on the ship that would take him back home, but he found that his cabin had been given to another passenger. There was nothing to be done, he was told. Douglass decided that he would still take the journey, sleeping without a private cabin for the trip. On April 20, after a little more than two weeks at sea, Douglass found himself back in the United States.

Within a few weeks of returning to the U.S., Douglass attended the annual convention of the American Anti-Slavery Society, which was held in New York City in May.

Douglass had written letters to Garrison that were published in the *Liberator* while he was away, and his fame had grown even while he was out of the country. He agreed to speak at the convention on May 11. Garrison rose to introduce his protégé, but the crowd of more than three thousand people was so eager to hear Douglass talk that they interrupted Garrison and began chanting for Douglass to speak.

Douglass's growing renown began to cause tension within the abolitionist movement. To make matters worse, Douglass had begun to consider the possibility of starting his own abolitionist newspaper. He enjoyed touring and speaking, but he also took pride in his ability to develop strong arguments against slavery and put them into writing. He had known ever since hearing Hugh Auld's opposition to teaching him to read and write that words could be powerful. Furthermore, Douglass thought it was important to show that a black man could succeed as a writer and editor. Most white Americans believed that blacks were simply not as intelligent as whites. Douglass thought that he could help prove them wrong by starting a paper that would show to the world what a black man was capable of.

Douglass's friends in Great Britain had enthusiastically supported his plan to start a paper, and they had collected about $2,500 to help him get started. He expected to find that his allies in the United States would be just as happy. Instead, he found that they were opposed to the idea. For one thing, they told him, there were already quite a few antislavery papers, including Garrison's *Liberator*. It was not clear that there were enough readers to support another paper. For another thing, they warned, it was very hard to make a paper work. Printing was expensive, and subscribers were hard to find. Finally, they worried that working as an editor would take away from Douglass's value as a speaker. It would surely be hard to find time to write and edit a paper while also continuing his busy lecture schedule.

For the moment, Douglass agreed to put off the paper, but he kept it in mind, still believing that it would work. That summer, Douglass and Garrison embarked on a speaking tour together, traveling from town to town in Pennsylvania and Ohio to rally support to the antislavery cause. The two men were now virtually equal in their fame. It was quite a change from the day in 1841 when Garrison had risen at a small meeting in New Bedford to thank Douglass for speaking. Douglass still remembered how he had been thrilled to come across the *Liberator*, to find that someone else was arguing so passionately against slavery.

Unfortunately for the two friends, their lecture tour proved to be the last time they met as close friends. While in Cleveland, Garrison became so ill that he decided to stay with friends there while he recovered, leaving Douglass to go ahead without him. He had talked to Douglass earlier in the summer about Douglass's hopes of starting a newspaper, and he thought they had agreed that it was best that Douglass continue to work as a speaker. Douglass, however, could not get the newspaper out of his mind. By the time Garrison recovered, Frederick had decided to pursue the paper despite Garrison's opposition. Garrison was hurt when he heard about the decision. Douglass had not even told him in person. In fact, as far as Garrison knew, Douglass had made no attempt once he left Cleveland to find out whether Garrison had recovered from his illness. After everything he had done for Douglass, Garrison had trouble forgiving him.

Meanwhile, Douglass believed that some of his friends in abolitionist circles opposed his attempt to start a paper because they did not think a black man could succeed at the task. And perhaps he knew that if he consulted Garrison before going ahead with the paper, the older man would be able to talk him out of it. Once Douglass made up his mind and informed the Anti-Slavery Society, the organization that he had worked for since 1841 told him that it would no longer employ him as a speaker.

With the *Liberator* already firmly established in Boston, Douglass decided that it might be best to publish his paper elsewhere, even though it would mean uprooting his family for a new home. He moved to Rochester, in western New York. Like Boston, upstate New York was home to quite a few prominent abolitionists, including a wealthy philanthropist named Gerrit Smith, the man who had run for president as a member of the Liberty Party in 1840. Douglass soon became close friends with Smith, and Smith was always generous in lending financial support to Douglass's new venture as a newspaper editor.

On December 3, 1847, Douglass published the first issue of his paper. He named it the *North Star*, after the bright star that guided runaway slaves on their journey north. Douglass found, as Garrison and others had warned him, that publishing a newspaper was not an easy undertaking. Even when the circulation grew to about 3,000 subscribers, that was not always enough to pay for the expenses of printing the paper.

Despite the struggle, Douglass was proud of his paper, and now that he was no longer part of the abolitionist circle in Boston, he found his outlook on the struggle to end slavery changing. In Rochester, he came across people with different approaches to the antislavery movement. He had always

# THE NORTH STAR.

RIGHT IS OF NO SEX—TRUTH IS OF NO COLOR—GOD IS THE FATHER OF US ALL, AND ALL WE ARE BRETHREN.

VOL. I. NO. 23.  ROCHESTER, N. Y., FRIDAY, JUNE 2, 1848.  WHOLE NO. 23.

## Communication.

### REV. JOHN LELAND.

### Selections.

Beneath the masthead of Frederick Douglass's newspaper the *North Star* is the paper's motto: Right is of No Sex—Truth is of No Color—God is the Father of Us All, And All We are Brethren. *(Courtesy of the Library of Congress)*

believed the only way to end slavery was by persuading Americans that it was immoral. But he also had experienced firsthand how important slavery was in the South, and how deeply many whites in the North believed that blacks were inferior. Gradually, Douglass began to reconsider whether moral arguments alone would be enough to end slavery.

Not long after he moved to Rochester, Douglass met one man who made a deep impression on him.

While traveling through western Massachusetts, he was invited to visit John Brown. Douglass had heard of Brown before, but he had not met him. Brown was known within the abolitionist movement for his strong opposition to slavery and his serious demeanor. Brown lived with his family in a small, plain house that was empty of luxuries, despite Brown's success as a merchant. After Douglass and the Brown family finished eating dinner, Brown took Douglass aside to talk to him about a plan he had been working on for some time.

Brown began by discussing his heartfelt hatred of slavery. Slaveholders, he told Douglass, had committed a crime by enslaving their fellow human beings, and they deserved to be held accountable for their deeds. He believed that slaves had the right to do whatever it took to gain their freedom, even if it meant killing their masters. Brown believed that violence was inevitable in the fight against slavery—there was no chance that slaveholders could be convinced to give up their valuable property without force.

Then Brown told Douglass that he was developing a plan to help slaves escape. He wanted to start a colony of slaves in the mountains of western Virginia. He would help slaves escape from their masters, and they could subsequently hide in the mountains, take up arms, and fight the slave owners.

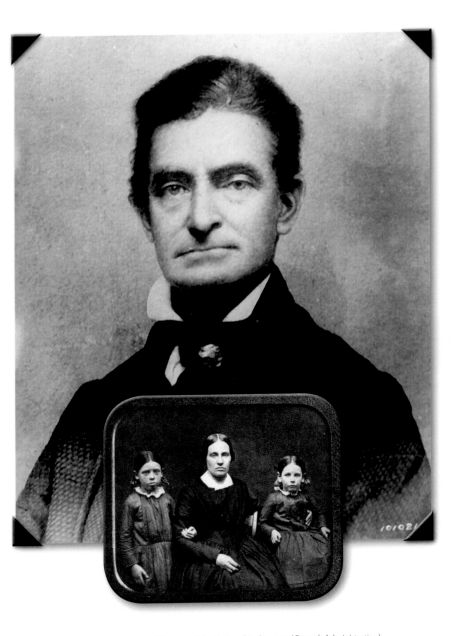

John Brown, circa 1856 *(Courtesy of the National Archives and Records Administration)*

Inset: Brown's second wife, Mary Ann, with two of their thirteen children.
*(Courtesy of the Library of Congress)*

Hidden away in the mountains, he said, it would be hard for the slaveholders to find and defeat them. He hoped to put his plan into action with about twenty-five armed men. He would march them into the mountains and then send them down on occasional raids on nearby farms.

Douglass saw that Brown had clearly thought through this plan, but he was skeptical that it could work. Still, Brown's conviction regarding the necessity of force almost convinced Douglass. He began to doubt that it was possible to bring about the end of slavery without the use of violence. From then on, he no longer agreed with Garrison and many of his friends in the abolitionist movement that only peaceful means should be used to combat slavery.

In the summer of 1848, Douglass began to change his mind about the use of politics against slavery as well. He took part in a women's rights convention held in the town of Seneca Falls in northern New York. The meeting was organized by a famous activist named Elizabeth Cady Stanton, who had long been a supporter of both abolitionism and women's rights. Women had always played an important role in the antislavery movement, but they were often prevented from speaking by their male counterparts. For some women, their involvement in abolitionism inspired them to start calling for women's rights as well.

The attendees of the conference approved a document, the Declaration of Sentiments, that declared that women should have the same rights as men—including the right to vote. They modeled the document on the Declaration of Independence, stating that:

> " We hold these truths to be self-evident: that all men and women are created equal; that they are endowed by their Creator with certain inalienable rights; that among these are life, liberty, and the pursuit of happiness; that to secure these rights governments are instituted, deriving their just powers from the consent of the governed. "

Elizabeth Cady Stanton *(Courtesy of the Seneca Falls Historical Society)*

Then, just as the Declaration of Independence had listed complaints against the King of England, the Declaration of Sentiments listed a number of complaints against the way men treated women in American society, including the fact that women were not allowed to vote.

Douglass supported these resolutions, although he had never believed that change would come about through politics. But seeing the importance of voting to these women might have helped change his mind. That fall, he began to be more active in politics, partly through his friendship with Gerrit Smith. Douglass had always thought that it was necessary to compromise too much to succeed in politics, and he was not willing to compromise on the issue of slavery. But as he began to attend Liberty Party meetings, he realized that he might as well do his best to shape the party so that it took a hard antislavery stand.

Slavery was one of several factors causing an upheaval of American politics. Two parties—the Democrats and the Whigs—had dominated politics since the 1830s, but both parties were changing because of slavery. As slavery became an important political issue, the differences between the slave states and the free states grew. In 1848, there were still few whites in the North who wanted to end slavery, but there was a growing number of whites who were concerned about the spread of slavery. It was fine for slavery to continue in the South, they felt, but they did not want to see it extended farther to the west, and they certainly did not want to have to compete with slave labor in the North.

Meanwhile, white Southerners began to feel under attack from the North. The constant harassment of slave owners by abolitionists convinced white Southerners that they had to spread slavery—otherwise, they worried, the North would eventually abolish it.

With his interest in politics growing, Douglass attended a convention held in the fall of 1848 in Buffalo, New York. The purpose of this gathering was to create a new political party, the Free Soil Party. The goal of those at the meeting was to create a party that would appeal to a wide range of white Northerners, whether they were abolitionists or not. The Liberty Party held limited appeal for many whites, because they felt it was too radical in its opposition to slavery. The Free Soil Party did not take a strong stand against slavery where it already existed, but it opposed allowing slavery to be extended

MARRIAGE OF THE FREE SOIL AND LIBERTY PARTIES.

The alliance between Free Soil Democrats and Whigs and the more extremist abolitionist Liberty party is lampooned in this 1848 political cartoon. The comical portrayal shows the wedding of Free Soil presidential candidate Martin Van Buren (center left) and a ragged black woman (center right). Van Buren says, "I find that politics, as well as poverty, make one acquainted with strange bedfellows." (*Courtesy of the Library of Congress*)

as new states joined the Union. That fall, the new party ran a candidate in the presidential election. The candidate, Martin Van Buren, had little chance of winning, but Douglass believed that it was still an important step in the fight against slavery. More and more whites were becoming part of the antislavery movement, even if they did not all agree on every issue.

The Free Soil Party was unsuccessful in the election, winning few votes, as most white Americans voted on issues other than slavery. It would not be long, however, before slavery was at the center of the political stage.

In 1847, the United States defeated Mexico in a war fought over a territorial dispute. As part of the agreement ending the war, the United States purchased an enormous amount of land, including territory from what is now Texas all the way to California. By 1850, California was applying to become a state, and that could upset the delicate balance of political power. California had adopted a constitution that would make it a free state, which angered southern politicians. At the time, there were fifteen slaves states and fifteen free states, which meant that there was an equal number of senators from both the North and the South. If California were admitted, the North would gain an edge in the Senate. One southern senator, John C. Calhoun, threatened that southern states might be forced to secede from the Union if California became a free state, and he demanded a constitutional amendment protecting the rights of slaveholders.

Northern politicians had no intention of allowing the Union to be broken or of amending the Constitution, so they tried to find a compromise that would allow California to become a state while easing the South's worries. In the legislation that resulted, California was admitted, and in return the South was able to pass a stronger fugitive slave law, which would make

Martin Van Buren
*(Courtesy of the Library of Congress)*

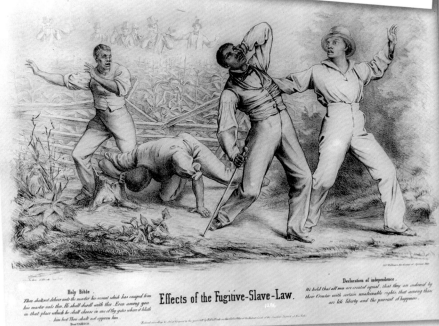

Top: Political cartoon attacking abolitionism
Bottom: A political cartoon condemning the Fugitive Slave Act
passed by Congress in 1850 *(Courtesy of the Library of Congress)*

it even harder for slaves to escape from slavery. This new law required northern states to help slave owners recapture runaway slaves, and it strengthened the penalties for anyone in the North who helped slaves escape. If a black man or woman was captured in the North and charged with being a runaway, they would not even be allowed to testify in their own defense. Instead, a commissioner appointed by the federal government would decide the case.

Douglass, like many Northerners both black and white, was outraged by this bill. He knew the terror of running away, and he also knew how hard it was to live in the North under the fear of being recaptured. Of course, with the help of his friends, he had been able to purchase his official freedom and now no longer had to worry about being returned to slavery, but he remembered the fear he had felt while wandering the streets of New York City after his escape. Since his move to Rochester, Douglass had begun using his home as a haven for runaway slaves. The tired runaways were able to spend a night at the Douglass household, and the next day Douglass would send them on their way to Canada and give them money for their journey. After the passage of the fugitive slave law, many runaway slaves in the North began to flee to Canada, because they worried that they might be recaptured if they remained in the U.S.

In 1851, three black men in Pennsylvania killed a slave owner who was trying to return them to slavery. The men quickly fled farther north, soon making their way to Rochester, where they stayed for a few hours at the Douglass house. Douglass knew that if the men were tracked to his home, it would result in an armed confrontation. When night fell, he loaded the men into his carriage and drove them to the landing where they could board a ship bound for Canada.

The next year, Douglass and his family moved to a farm about two miles south of Rochester. Its rural location near Canada made it an ideal stop for slaves on their way farther north. With its large number of antislavery activists, Rochester was a popular stop on the Underground Railroad.

Even before the uproar over the fugitive slave law, Douglass had been reconsidering his ideas about politics, violence, and abolitionism. The experiences of runaway slaves in the years after 1850 made him more convinced that it would not be enough just to argue against the immorality of slavery. It would take political action, and perhaps even force, to bring slavery to an end.

# Chapter 8
# The Constitution Question

By 1852, the United States was well on its way to war. Americans did not know at the time that disagreements over slavery would eventually result in conflict on the battlefield, but they knew that it was becoming harder and harder to ignore the differences between the North and South. For Frederick Douglass, the dispute over slavery was about more than slavery itself—it was also about the place of black Americans in the United States.

On that issue, Douglass was torn. He believed that the United States was his home as much as it was the home of any white man or woman, but he had also experienced rejection in both the North and South when he tried to claim that he, and other blacks, deserved all the rights of whites.

The Fourth of July always made Douglass feel this confusion more strongly than any other day. So when he was invited to give a speech on July 4, 1852, by a women's antislavery society in Rochester, he saw it as his chance to explain this confusion to white Americans. The result was the most memorable speech of his long life.

Douglass had replied to the antislavery group that he would give the speech, but that he preferred to speak on the fifth of July rather than on the holiday itself. Hundreds of listeners crowded into Corinthian Hall in Rochester to hear him speak. Douglass had spent weeks preparing the speech. He wanted to make sure he took full advantage of this opportunity.

Douglass had now been a professional speaker for more than a decade. Despite his years of lectures and writing, however, on this day he felt nervous. He spoke quietly at first, and, as he often did, he apologized for not speaking as eloquently as he would have liked to speak. His voice grew louder as he continued. He began by reminding his audience that the Fourth of July had a very different meaning for slaves than for white Americans. For whites, it was a reminder of the heroism of the country's Founding Fathers and of their efforts to escape oppression. He said that those men had, indeed, been brave.

Then Douglass turned his attention to the present. He argued that Americans had lost the spirit of the American Revolution—they had forgotten the ideals celebrated by Washington, Jefferson, and the other Founding Fathers. The Fourth of July, he said, was not a holiday for him or other black Americans. White Americans excluded them from celebrating the heritage of the Revolution. "The blessings in which you, this day, rejoice, are not enjoyed in common," Douglass declared. "This Fourth July is yours, not mine. You may rejoice, I must mourn." Douglass reminded his listeners that while they celebrated their freedom, millions of Americans remained enslaved. Slavery, he said, proved that Americans were hypocrites when it came to freedom.

"What, to the American slave, is your Fourth of July?" he asked. "I answer: a day that reveals to him, more than all other days of the year, the gross injustice and cruelty to which he is the constant victim. To him your celebration is a sham." What would it take, Douglass asked, before white Americans accepted that blacks were their equals? "Must I undertake to prove that the slave is a man? That point is conceded already. Nobody doubts it."

After listing the cruelties of slavery, Douglass said that he still had hope. He still believed that the spirit of the American Revolution was on the side of the slaves. Then, he said something that would have shocked William Lloyd Garrison and many other abolitionists. "Interpreted as it ought to be interpreted," he said, "the Constitution is a glorious liberty document."

Many abolitionists, and probably most white Americans, believed that the Constitution protected slavery. Douglass himself had long believed that, too. But he had changed his mind. Finally, Douglass ended his speech by predicting that slavery would end. "The doom of slavery is certain. I, therefore, leave off where I began, with hope. While drawing encouragement from the Declaration of Independence, the great principles it contains, and the genius of American institutions, my spirit is also cheered by the obvious tendencies of the age."

Douglass's changing opinion of the Constitution reflected a long process of thinking about the place of black Americans in the United States. For years, he had agreed with the Garrisonians that the Constitution supported slavery. But it was important to Douglass to prove that that was not true, because he believed that he belonged in the United States. He did not want to destroy American institutions; he wanted to expand them so that everyone could be included.

The debate over the Constitution involved looking closely at what the authors of the Constitution had included in the document. The Constitution was written in 1787, at a time when the United States was struggling to survive as an independent nation. It had won its freedom from England with the end of the American Revolution in 1783, but it was still not clear that the country would be able to govern itself. The problem was finding a way to get people from thirteen very different states to agree on a single national government. As a result, creating the Constitution involved making a lot of compromises.

In May 1787, fifty-five men met in Philadelphia to create a new framework to govern the country. They included representatives from every state except Rhode Island. For the next few months, they argued over a number of difficult issues, including the future of slavery. A few northern representatives hoped to use the new Constitution to put an end to slavery, but delegates from southern states would not agree. In the end, the Constitution remained somewhat ambiguous when it came to this important issue.

Many abolitionists, such as William Lloyd Garrison, pointed to two sections of the Constitution that they believed supported slavery. One section of the document seemed to protect the rights of slaveholders to capture a slave who escaped:

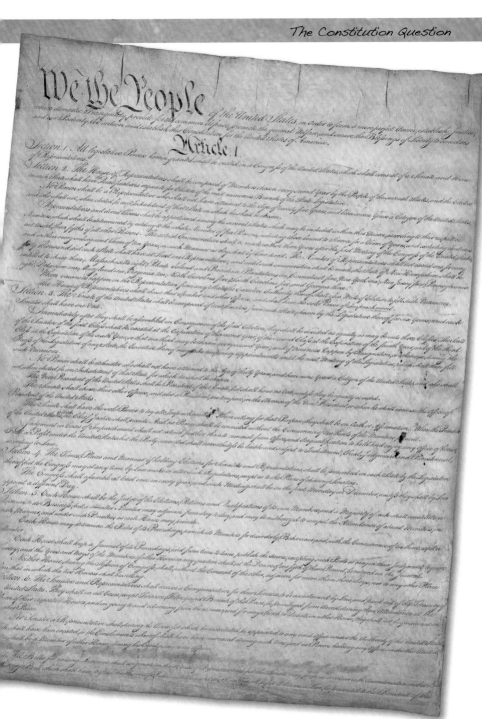

The United States Constitution
(Courtesy of the National Archives and Records Administration)

*No person held to Service or Labour in one State, under the Laws thereof, escaping into another, shall, in Consequence of any Law or Regulation therein, be discharged from such Service or Labour, But shall be delivered up on claim of the Party to whom such service or Labour may be due.*

What that meant, as Douglass often reminded his audiences throughout the 1840s, was that a slave who escaped from slavery could still be claimed by the former owner.

Douglass also liked to point out another section of the Constitution. To determine how many representatives in the U.S. House of Representatives a state would receive, the Constitution used the number of free citizens of the state plus three-fifths of the number of slaves (although the Constitution did not actually use the word slave), an equation known as the three-fifths compromise. As a result, Douglass reminded his audiences that "every man that takes part in the American Constitution, that regards himself as a citizen of the United States, is bound by the Constitution to uphold and sustain American slavery."

Douglass often argued that to end slavery, it would be necessary to break apart the United States. He had been encouraged in this view by Garrison, who strongly believed that the Union was not worth saving.

The longer Douglass remained in Rochester, the more he began to question his earlier arguments against slavery. He still believed, as Garrison did, that slavery was immoral and that it would take a change in the mind of the public to bring it to an end, but he also felt that it might be worthwhile to use other tools as well.

Perhaps the Constitution could be one of those tools. Douglass knew that Americans held great regard for important documents such as the Constitution and the Declaration of Independence. If he could convince them that those documents did not support slavery—that, in fact, they should be regarded as antislavery—then maybe he could win more converts to the abolitionist cause.

Frederick Douglass, 1856

In his speeches and writings, Douglass began to focus on the parts of the Constitution that talked about freedom and justice, rather than on the isolated passages that seemed to support slavery.

In 1851, Douglass officially announced his change of view in an article in the *North Star*. The Constitution, he wrote, should not be used to support slavery. His former allies in the abolitionist movement did not take his change of mind well. Members of the American Anti-Slavery Society passed a resolution. Every member of the society, it declared, must condemn the Constitution. Douglass was undeterred by this opposition. He no longer had to convince his fellow Americans to overthrow the government. He just had to convince them to live up to the ideals of their current government.

Despite his change of heart, Douglass wanted to continue to be active with as many antislavery organizations as possible. In 1853, he spoke at the meetings of both the American Anti-Slavery Society and the American and Foreign Anti-Slavery Society (AFASA), two groups that often clashed over abolitionist tactics. Douglass titled his speech at the AFASA meeting "A Nation in the Midst of a Nation." He had been invited to speak by Lewis Tappan, a leader of the AFASA. The Broadway tabernacle was filled for this speech, including many black Americans. The meeting began at 7:30 in the evening, and Douglass took the stage soon thereafter.

Douglass talked about how different the country looked to black Americans than to white Americans. Most black Americans had been born in the U.S., Douglass said, yet they were looked at as foreigners by whites. "The glorious doctrines of your revolutionary fathers, and the still more glorious teachings of the Son of God, are construed and applied against us," he said. He added that the country seemed to ignore the principles of the Constitution and the Declaration of Independence when it came to blacks.

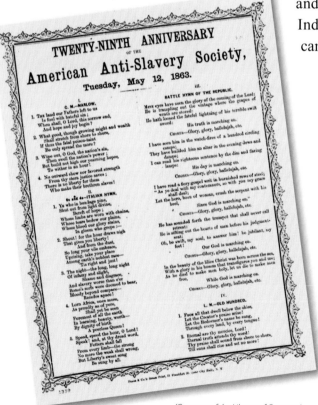

*(Courtesy of the Library of Congress)*

Douglass mentioned that politicians had tried to keep any discussion of slavery out of politics and to try to extend the reach of slavery through war and the fugitive slave law. He also mentioned the resurgence of the American Colonization Party, which had started around 1818 in an attempt to remove blacks from the country and establish a country in Africa for them. The American Colonization Society lost steam by the 1830s, but in the 1850s it began to gain appeal again as whites tried to figure out what to do with the millions of black Americans in their midst. State governments in both the North and South began to give money to the cause of African emigration, believing as Thomas Jefferson had written that whites and blacks could never coexist peacefully. That was what Douglass was arguing against. He believed that the United States was the home of black Americans, too, not just white Americans.

Blacks were gaining ground in the North, Douglass said, accumulating wealth and becoming an integral part of society. And that, he said, was what worried white Northerners. Whites were fine with blacks as long as they were kept at the bottom of society, but whites began to object as blacks moved up the social ladder.

Just as Douglass spoke to whites about the need to accept blacks and to treat them equally, he also spoke to his fellow black Americans about the need to be productive members of society. He began to work to establish a school for black Americans that would teach them basic skills, such as reading and writing, and to train them for work in fields such as agriculture and industry.

A third goal of his was to prove that blacks were the equal of whites in every respect. That was one reason he had been so determined to start his own paper. He wanted to show that a black man could succeed in this difficult and competitive field. That was also why he had grown tired of making the same speech over and over again during his early years with the American Anti-Slavery Society. He didn't want to repeat the same arguments time and again.

On July 12, 1854, he gave a speech in Ohio addressing this issue. Douglass thought it very important to speak well, so he spent weeks preparing the speech. The speech came during graduation week at Western Reserve College in Hudson, Ohio. Douglass became the first black person to give a keynote address at a major U.S. university. Some of the faculty, and even the president of the college, tried to withdraw the invitation given to Douglass to speak by the graduating class. Almost 3,000 people listened to the speech, which began at approximately one o'clock. The listeners were not all friendly to his argument, but the speech was generally well received. A local paper commented that the listeners listened closely, despite the heat and the length of the speech—two hours. Some in the audience even cried.

Douglass planned to discuss the basis on which blacks were considered inferior, but before going into that part of the speech, he began by saying that it was impossible even for scholars to be neutral on the question of slavery. It was cowardly, he said, to avoid deciding for yourself whether slavery was wrong or right, regardless of your opinion on the inferiority of blacks.

Douglass then quoted from an article in the *Richmond Examiner*, a newspaper published in Richmond, Virginia, that discussed the question of the rights of blacks. The paper said that the reasons blacks were not eligible for the rights listed

The chapel of Western Reserve Academy in Hudson, Ohio (*Courtesy of Zach Vesoulis*)

in the Declaration of Independence was that black men were not men in the same way that white men were.

Douglass said that it was ridiculous to have to answer such a claim, as it seemed obvious that he and other blacks were, indeed, human beings. "Men instinctively distinguish between men and brutes," he said. "Common sense itself is scarcely needed to detect the absence of manhood in a donkey, or to recognize its presence in a negro."

Douglass argued that slaveholders had enslaved blacks, and then used the fact that blacks were slaves to argue that they were only fit to be slaves. Douglass also argued that the accomplishments of the ancient Egyptians were proof that blacks were not inherently inferior. Douglass argued that the only reason that blacks appeared in any way inferior in the United States was that they had been enslaved for hundreds of years.

Then Douglass went on to discuss the three possible ways that the United States might rid itself of all blacks. There was colonization, which he said was impossible because America was the native home of blacks; extermination, which he also considered unlikely; and dying out, which seemed unlikely. The only question, Douglass said, was whether blacks would be accepted into American society and given the chance to contribute or would be continually enslaved and removed from the rest of society.

In just a few short years, that question would be answered.

# Chapter
# 9
# An Escalating Conflict

❧⟡❧

In the mid-1850s, the battle over slavery heated up. The Whig Party had fallen apart; Northerners felt that it supported slavery too strongly, and white Southerners believed that it did not support slavery strongly enough. Meanwhile, the Democratic Party, which had always had a lot of support among slaveholders, continued to grow stronger in the South and weaker in the North. The abolitionists had succeeded in making slavery a national issue. They could no longer be ignored.

The Compromise of 1850 temporarily settled the question of how to admit a new state, but by 1854 the problem arose again. Congress had to decide what to do with the Nebraska Territory, a large chunk of land to the west of Missouri. After some debate, Congress decided that the territory would be split into two—Nebraska and Kansas—and eventually those territories would be allowed to apply to join the Union as states. When the territories applied for statehood, their residents would vote on whether or not to allow slavery. The soil and climate of Nebraska—the more northern of the territories—made it unlikely that it would become a slave state, so both proslavery and antislavery Americans focused their attention on Kansas. Would it decide to enter the Union as a free state or as a slave state?

Soon, thousands of settlers from both the North and South were making their way to Kansas to take part in the elections that would decide the future of the territory. The proslavery side had the edge at first, as whites from Missouri crossed the border to vote, helping to elect a proslavery legislature. As more antislavery settlers arrived, they created their own government. By 1856, there were two different legislatures competing to be recognized as the legitimate governments of Kansas.

With large numbers of men—most of them armed—now in the territory, it did not take long for the conflict to become violent. At the center of the conflict was the man who had so impressed Frederick Douglass years before: John Brown. After a group of proslavery settlers attacked the antislavery town of Lawrence, Kansas, Brown led an attack on proslavery settlers, killing five men. The violence continued to grow worse.

Throughout this upheaval, Douglass continued to publish his paper and travel around the North speaking against slavery.

The conflict in Kansas convinced him that bringing slavery to an end might require even more violence. "It is, I think, pretty well settled, that liberty and slavery cannot dwell in the United States in peaceful relations," he declared in a speech in Chicago, Illinois. "The South must either give up slavery, or the North must give up liberty."

In his speeches, Douglass tried to convince his listeners that it was not just black Americans who suffered from slavery. Whites, too, he argued, gave up some of their liberties when they allowed slaveholders to control national politics and stifle those who spoke out against slavery. And, he warned, it would not be long before slaveholders would try to extend the reach of slavery across the country—even to the North. By this time, Douglass was more confident in his position that the Constitution did not support slavery, and he proclaimed to his audiences that they had to end slavery if they wanted to live up to the lofty ideals of the Founding Fathers. He often quoted from the Declaration of Independence to remind his listeners of what it promised.

In 1857, the Supreme Court delivered a decision that frustrated Douglass's efforts to create a society where whites and blacks could live as equals. The case involved a slave named Dred Scott. Scott had been taken by his owner to territories that barred slavery. He sued for his freedom, arguing that because he had spent time in those free territories, he should be declared a free man. The Supreme Court sided with his owner, however, and ruled that he should remain a slave. The chief justice of the Supreme Court, Roger B. Taney, went even further. He wrote in his decision that because Scott was black, he was not a citizen of the United States. Even free blacks, Taney said, were not citizens. Taney also concluded that Congress could not ban slavery in any of the territories that had not yet been admitted as states. Many white Northerners were upset by the decision. It seemed that all the power of the federal government was behind the rights of slaveholders.

It did not take the Dred Scott decision to convince John Brown that something had to be done to stop slavery. In 1859, he led an attack on slavery that shocked the country. Frederick Douglass, however, was not surprised—he had been told about the plan by Brown in person.

Wood engraving of Dred Scott in *Century Magazine*, 1887 *(Courtesy of the Library of Congress)*

In late January 1858, Brown visited Douglass in Rochester. He told Douglass that he was working on the final plans to launch an attack in western Virginia. For the next year, Brown gathered support for his project. By the fall of 1859, he was ready, and to help him, he asked Douglass to visit him secretly in the town of Chambersburg, Pennsylvania.

Brown planned to launch his attack from there, but he had changed his mind about what he would do. When Douglass arrived in Pennsylvania, Brown told him that he now intended to attack Harpers Ferry, an army post in western Virginia. Douglass felt that this plan had little chance of success, but

111

Brown would not be discouraged. He even asked Douglass to join him, hoping that the presence of this leader would inspire slaves to flock to Harpers Ferry to become part of the attack. Douglass turned down the invitation. He admired Brown's courage, but he did not think the plan made much sense or had much chance for success.

John Brown, 1859
*(Courtesy of the Library of Congress)*

On October 16, Brown put his plan into action. Meanwhile, Douglass left Chambersburg to travel to Philadelphia, where he planned to give a speech on the eighteenth. Brown and nineteen other men made their way to Harpers Ferry and took control of the small arsenal. But U.S. Marines soon arrived and surrounded Brown. In the gunfight that followed, several of Brown's men were killed, and Brown himself was taken captive.

Douglass heard news of Brown's attack while in Philadelphia. "The announcement came upon us with the startling effect of an earthquake," he later wrote. He was not surprised to hear of Brown's capture, but he began to worry for his own safety when he heard that the governor of Virginia, Henry Wise, had asked the president to arrest anyone who had helped Brown carry out his venture. Wise had even named Douglass as one of those suspected of being involved in Brown's plot. That's because when Brown was captured, a note from Douglass, written in 1857, was found on him, implicating Douglass in the attack.

Top: Harpers Ferry, 1865 (*Courtesy of the National Archives and Records Administration*)

Bottom: *Harper's Weekly* illustration of John Brown's fort under attack
(*Courtesy of the National Park Service*)

After giving his speech on the eighteenth, Douglass quickly decided that he had to make it farther north to escape possible capture. Fortunately for Douglass, he had friends to help him escape. When a telegram arrived in Philadelphia instructing the county sheriff to arrest Douglass, the telegraph operator, James Hern, delayed delivering the telegram. He rushed first to the house where Douglass was staying to let him know of the danger. Only after making sure that Douglass was on his way out of the city did Hern deliver the telegram. Douglass realized that Brown had left a number of important papers at Douglass's home in Rochester. He gave a friend instructions to send a telegram to his son, telling him to put the papers in a secure place.

Douglass traveled by carriage to Patterson, New Jersey, where he boarded a train to Rochester. Even in Rochester, however, he was nervous about his safety. Governor Wise was still eager to arrest Douglass and charge him in connection with Brown. Other men who had provided money or assistance to Brown had already fled to Canada. Douglass decided that he, too, should go to Canada for the time being. The day after he left, federal marshals arrived in Rochester to arrest him. Douglass had left just in time.

Once in Canada, Douglass decided that now was the perfect time to leave for a long-planned trip to Europe. On November 12, 1859, he left for England from Nova Scotia. He stayed first with friends in the city of Halifax, where he spent the Christmas holiday. Although he had long looked forward to a second trip abroad, he began his trip depressed about the state of the battle against slavery. It seemed to him that the slave power was at its height. The president supported slavery, Congress refused to act against it, and the Supreme Court had ruled that black men and women were not American citizens. The journey itself only made his mood worse. There were stormy seas for the entire two-week trip. And on December 2, not long after Douglass arrived in England, the state of Virginia hanged John Brown.

The first time Douglass traveled to England, he had spent much of his time criticizing the United States. Now, a decade later, he found himself defending the country from the criticisms of British antislavery activists. In Scotland in late March, he gave a speech discussing his views of the Constitution. He started by outlining the position of the Garrisonians, pointing out that they viewed the Constitution as a proslavery document. Then Douglass argued that, in fact, the Constitution did not guarantee the right of slaveholders to keep their slaves. It was true, Douglass conceded, that some Americans chose to use the Constitution to defend slavery, but he believed that eventually the United States would live up to its promises and bestow freedom on every American.

Douglass's time in England was soon cut short. In March, he received a letter from his daughter Rosetta. She told him that Douglass's youngest daughter, Annie, had died on March 13. Douglass quickly decided to return home, despite the concern that he might still be arrested. When he arrived in Rochester, however, he found that by that time the government was more interested in trying to forget about John Brown than in remembering to arrest Frederick Douglass.

Douglass returned to the United States to find that the issue that had consumed his life—slavery—had now consumed the rest of the country as well. The upcoming presidential election was on the minds of many Americans. Never before had slavery been such a central concern in a presidential election.

The Democratic Party was now split. Democrats had lost much of their power in the North, and those who remained supported Illinois senator Stephen Douglas. But southern Democrats nominated their own candidate, John C. Breckinridge, who promised to extend slavery into the remaining territories and to annex Cuba as another slave state. Meanwhile, a new political party, the Republican Party, had been gaining strength in the North since the mid-1850s. In 1860, the party nominated Abraham Lincoln, a lawyer from Illinois. Lincoln and the Republicans were not abolitionists. They had no intention of opposing slavery where it already existed. But they did believe that it should remain limited to the states that already had slavery.

As the November election approached, the nation was on edge. Each of the candidates had support in only limited areas of the country. For the first time, a Republican was elected president. Lincoln won, but with just 40 percent of the popular vote. Breckenridge dominated the vote in the South, and Douglas picked up limited support in both the North and South.

Frederick Douglass was pleased with the outcome. He knew that Lincoln was not an abolitionist, but it was at least a far better choice for antislavery activists than Douglas or Breckenridge.

White Southerners, however, were outraged, and the nation waited to see if southern states would follow through on their threats to secede. In the North, some whites blamed the abolitionists for causing all this trouble. In early December, Douglass found out for himself that Lincoln's victory did not mean that everyone in the North opposed slavery. He planned to speak at a gathering to celebrate the memory of John Brown, but before he could even start his speech, a group of white protesters began shouting him down. They stood in his way as he tried to make it to the platform to speak, and he had to fight his way through the crowd.

Finally Douglass made his way to the stage and began to speak. At first the protesters simply yelled their complaints. Then they ran toward the stage, and a riot broke out. Chairs were flying, and men were fighting hand-to-hand as each side tried to overpower the other. The riot ended only when police arrived and began escorting the abolitionists out of the meeting hall.

Then, about three weeks later, on December 20, 1860, South Carolina seceded from the Union. Before Lincoln even took office, Alabama, Florida, Georgia, Louisiana, Mississippi, and Texas followed South Carolina's lead and also seceded. Even if the new president chose to try to keep the country together, it seemed war was inevitable. In early February, these states declared that they had formed an independent nation—the Confederate States of America. They even wrote their own constitution and elected a president, a wealthy slave owner named Jefferson Davis.

On March 4, Lincoln took office. He was now president of a deeply divided nation, including several states that believed that they were no longer part of the United States. In his inaugural address, Lincoln tried to reconcile the difference between North and South. He hoped at the very least to prevent any additional states from leaving the Union.

In early April, Lincoln faced his first test as president. He was notified that Fort Sumter, a Union post on an island off the coast of South Carolina, needed to be resupplied. If Lincoln sent supplies, the Confederacy could take it as an act of war. If he did not, the soldiers at the fort would be forced

President Abraham Lincoln and his Cabinet *(Courtesy of the Library of Congress)*

to surrender to the Confederacy. Lincoln tried to find a balance between supplying the troops and appeasing the South by sending only food and other basic supplies, leaving out any military supplies from the shipment. Nevertheless, the Confederacy took Lincoln's decision as an act of war, and on April 12 Confederate soldiers began shelling the fort. Within two days, the soldiers were forced to surrender.

In response, Lincoln requested that volunteers begin signing up to join the Army to put down this uprising. His actions convinced a number of other southern states that they, too, had to leave the Union. By the end of May, Arkansas, North Carolina, Tennessee, and Virginia had also seceded, and the country was at war.

# Chapter 10
# An American Citizen

The question now was why the North had gone to war. Was the purpose of the war simply to preserve the Union? Or was it to bring slavery to an end? Douglass took it upon himself to do everything he could to make sure that the war would not end without the emancipation of the 4 million black Americans enslaved in the South.

For Lincoln, the issue was more complicated. Four states that allowed slavery had not seceded—Delaware, Kentucky, Maryland, and Missouri. Lincoln worried that if those states did leave the Union, it would make winning the war

especially difficult. He believed that the primary purpose of the war was to preserve the Union, not to end slavery. He made it clear in his speeches that he would be willing to negotiate a truce that would allow the South to keep its slaves if the states would return to the Union.

Douglass soon grew frustrated with Lincoln's policies. He began to criticize Lincoln, arguing that freeing the slaves would take away millions of free laborers from the Confederacy. He believed that the war would eventually end slavery, but he saw no reason to put off the decision to free the slaves.

Abraham Lincoln
*(Courtesy of the Library of Congress)*

Gradually, Lincoln began to move toward Douglass's position. In April 1862, he signed a bill that ended slavery in Washington, D.C., something that had long been a goal of the abolitionists. Later that year, Lincoln made the decision to free the slaves. On July 22, 1862, Lincoln informed the members of his Cabinet that he intended to issue a declaration that would abolish slavery in the states that had rebelled. His advisers warned him that it would be better to wait until after a Union victory to make the announcement, otherwise it might appear to be an act of desperation.

Neither side had been able to gain a decisive edge. The North had the advantage in the number of men of military age and in the ability to produce all the weapons and ammunition needed to wage a war, but the South had the advantage of geography. To win, the Confederacy did not need to conquer any territory. It only had to survive until the North grew tired of fighting. The North, however, had to invade the Confederacy to defeat it. The South won a number of early victories, bolstering its hope that it would be able to hold off the mighty North. By 1862, however, the North was beginning to have better fortune on the battlefields, and in September 1862 Union soldiers in northern Virginia won a bloody battle that allowed Lincoln to make his announcement.

After that battle, Lincoln declared that on the first day of 1863, he would free all the slaves in Confederate territory if those states did not end their rebellion before that time. However, Lincoln's declaration would not affect the slaves in the border states—those states that allowed slavery but had not seceded.

Douglass and other abolitionists were excited about Lincoln's decision, even if they worried that it did not do enough to abolish slavery entirely. As New Year's Day approached, they waited anxiously to find out whether Lincoln would follow through on his promise. On January 1, 1863, Lincoln issued the Emancipation Proclamation. The Civil War was now, in part, a war to end slavery.

Douglass's next goal was to convince Lincoln to allow black men to serve in the Army. He believed it was important for the nation to see black men fighting for their country, and, of course, it would add thousands of soldiers to the strength of the Union Army. Most northern whites opposed the idea of allowing black troops to fight. For one thing, there was a widely held belief that black men were too cowardly to make good soldiers. For another thing, they worried that allowing black men to fight would be a step toward social equality, and that was unthinkable.

Douglass did his best to counter those arguments. Give black men a chance, he said, and they would prove their courage and ability. After Lincoln issued his proclamation, the Army began to accept black recruits. Douglass now used his speeches and his paper to encourage black men to take this opportunity to enlist.

The governor of Massachusetts soon announced that he planned to raise two regiments of black soldiers, the Fifty-fourth and Fifty-fifth Massachusetts regiments. Encouraged, Douglass increased his efforts to convince black men to enlist. Among those who took his advice were his twenty-two-year-old son, Lewis, and his eighteen-year-old son, Charles, both of whom joined the Fifty-fourth. On May 18, 1863, a large crowd gathered in Boston to present the colors to the regiment as the soldiers prepared to ship out to islands off the coast of South Carolina.

These black soldiers faced a number of challenges. They were not paid as much as white soldiers, and they had trouble obtaining the supplies they needed. And for them, the fighting was even more dangerous that it was for white Union soldiers. The Confederacy declared that any black man caught as a soldier would be treated as a rebellious slave. In other words, if captured, black soldiers would not be given the rights of other prisoners of war. Instead, they would most likely be killed.

At first, there was widespread opposition within the Army to allow these new recruits to do anything other than manual labor. But in mid-July, the Fifty-fourth Massachusetts Regiment had a chance to prove its mettle. On July 18, the troops led the charge against Fort Wagner, a heavily defended Confederate fort in South Carolina. Lewis Douglass was among those who took part in the fight. "Men fell all around me," he wrote in a letter. "A shell would explode and clear a space of twenty feet, our men would close up again, but it was no use we had to retreat, which was a very hazardous undertaking. How I got out of that fight alive I cannot tell." The Union soldiers did not take the fort, but the members of the Fifty-fourth did succeed in showing that they deserved the chance to fight. Because of their bravery, thousands more black men were soon fighting as part of the Union Army.

With the bravery of the Fifty-fourth proved at Fort

Top: The storming of Fort Wagner *(Courtesy of the Library of Congress)* Bottom: The Battle of Olustee

Wagner, Douglass began to agitate to ensure that black soldiers were given the same pay and protection as white soldiers. After being asked by a white officer to help raise more recruits, Douglass replied that he could not do so until he was convinced that black soldiers would receive better treatment.

In the summer of 1863, Douglass had the chance to make that request to President Lincoln himself. Despite all his accomplishments, Douglass found himself getting nervous as his scheduled appointment with Lincoln approached. But when he was escorted into Lincoln's office, the president put him at ease immediately. Lincoln shook Douglass's hand and welcomed him, and then the two men began to talk about the role of black soldiers.

Douglass told the president that many black men were reluctant to join the Army because they believed that they would not be treated fairly. They were not paid as well as whites, they could not be promoted to become officers, and they were not protected by the same rules of war as whites. Lincoln replied that the unequal pay had been started to make it easier to convince white soldiers to fight alongside blacks, but that he hoped that soon the pay would be made equal.

Lincoln said that the issue of the Confederacy's announcement that they would treat captured black soldiers as slaves was more difficult. It was a hard decision to retaliate in an equal manner against captured Confederate soldiers, he said. Douglass left the meeting deeply impressed by the president. Douglass had not received all the assurances he had wanted, but he had faith that Lincoln would do what he could for black soldiers. He would never forget this meeting and the respect shown to him by the president.

It was also in the summer of 1863 that the war began to turn to the North's advantage. The Union won an important victory at Gettysburg, Pennsylvania, in early July. The North's superiority in population and industry was slowly giving it a decisive edge. As the war dragged on, Douglass began to talk more and more about the fate of black Americans once it finally ended.

In the spring of 1865, after four long years, the war came to an end. Douglass's son Lewis was stationed with his regiment in Maryland at the time, and he wrote to his father to tell him about an unexpected encounter. Lewis had walked eight miles from his post to the town of St. Michaels, where Douglass had lived with the Aulds. When he made it to the town, a woman came up to him and introduced herself. Lewis soon found out that he was talking to Eliza, his father's oldest sister. Eliza took Lewis around town and introduced him to a number of his cousins.

Douglass celebrated the end of the war, but the victory was soon tarnished. On April 14, Abraham Lincoln was shot while watching a play at Ford's Theater in Washington, D.C., and he died the next morning. His death added to the enormous number of casualties. More than 600,000 soldiers had died over the course of the war.

Still, something great had been achieved. In December 1865, the Thirteenth Amendment to the Constitution forever banned slavery in the United States. In the years after the war, the country ratified two additional constitutional amendments. The Fourteenth Amendment declared that blacks had the same rights of citizenship as whites, and the Fifteenth Amendment gave black men the right to vote.

These amendments helped the newly freed slaves make some progress, but Douglass worried that they would not be given equal opportunities. The federal government soon created the Freedmen's Bureau, which was intended to help the

Thirty-Eighth Congress of the United States of America;

At the Second Session,

Begun and held at the City of Washington, on Monday, the fifth day of December, one thousand eight hundred and sixty-four.

## A RESOLUTION

Submitting to the legislatures of the several States a proposition to amend the Constitution of the United States.

Resolved by the Senate and House of Representatives of the United States of America in Congress assembled, (two-thirds of both houses concurring), That the following article be proposed to the legislatures of the several States as an amendment to the Constitution of the United States, which, when ratified by three-fourths of said Legislatures, shall be valid, to all intents and purposes, as a part of the said Constitution, namely: Article XIII. Section 1. Neither slavery nor involuntary servitude, except as a punishment for crime whereof the party shall have been duly convicted, shall exist within the United States, or any place subject to their jurisdiction. Section 2. Congress shall have power to enforce this article by appropriate legislation.

Schuyler Colfax
Speaker of the House of Representatives

H. Hamlin
Vice President of the United States
and President of the Senate

Abraham Lincoln

Approved, February 1, 1865.

The Thirteenth Amendment to the U.S. Constitution

freed slaves get their start as free laborers. The new president, Andrew Johnson, hindered these efforts. He pardoned many former Confederate leaders, allowing them to regain their large plantations. In many areas, freed slaves were forced to work as sharecroppers. The white landowners continued to own the land, and would rent it to black farmers in return for some of the crops. The conditions of these agreements usually were in favor of the landowners, which meant that the former slaves often had little more money or power than they had had as slaves.

With the war over, some abolitionists decided that their efforts, too, were at an end. William Lloyd Garrison announced that he would stop publication of his paper, the *Liberator*, at the end of 1865, after publishing it every week since 1831. Douglass realized that there was still much left to do, however, including ensuring that the end of slavery actually brought about equality. But he was not sure what role he would play in this new struggle. He even wondered if he would be able to find work to do. He felt too old to return to a life of manual labor, but he did not know who would want to listen to an abolitionist now that slavery was ended. He soon found that many people were still interested in listening to what he had to say. He continued to give speeches to local organizations and universities, and he soon found himself making more money than he ever had before the Civil War.

The question was what he would talk about. Douglass turned much of his attention to the difficult problem of how to make American society work now that 4 million former slaves were free. Most whites, in both the North and South, continued to believe in their racial superiority.

Douglass learned from the experience of his children that the end of slavery had not brought about racial equality.

They struggled to find work, and even when they did have employment, they had to struggle against discrimination from white workers.

Douglass considered moving to the South to run for public office. His friends told him that he could surely win election to the House of Representatives if he moved to an area with a large black population. But Douglass felt that he was not quite the right type of person to be a politician. After all, he had never been good at making compromises. He did, however, begin spending more time farther to the south. He lobbied politicians to do more to give black men and women an equal opportunity to succeed. In 1870, he bought a large share of a newspaper, the *New National Era*, published in Washington, D.C. It was intended to provide important information for the growing number of black citizens living in the nation's capital.

Within a few years, Douglass and Anna made Washington, D.C., their home. They were spurred to move in part by Douglass's aspirations to be involved in national discussions about race and politics and in part by a devastating fire that destroyed their Rochester home in 1872. Lost in the fire was a complete set of Douglass's paper, the *North Star*—the only complete copy of the paper available anywhere. In addition to losing the paper, Douglass lost thousands of dollars of personal property. The Douglasses moved to a small house in Washington, and Douglass continued his work on the paper and in national politics.

In 1877, Douglass's hard work for the Republican Party was recognized when new president Rutherford B. Hayes, elected in 1876, appointed Douglass marshal of Washington, D.C. This was the first time that a black man had been given an office that had to be approved by a vote of the Senate. Most of Douglass's duties as marshal were ceremonial, and he had little power to affect policies taken by the president. But the position did give him a chance to provide a number of black men with jobs in the federal government, helping to build a strong black middle class in the nation's capital.

In the same year that Douglass took on his new role, he traveled to Maryland and made his way to St. Michaels. Thomas Auld, now not in good health, sent word through a friend that he would like to see his former slave. Douglass, nervous about the encounter but excited about the possibility, agreed. Douglass had mixed feelings about the meeting. He still remembered all the cruelties he had undergone as a slave—his time at Covey's, the lack of food, the whippings—but he also knew that if Auld had not sent him to work in Baltimore, it was likely that he would have remained a slave until the end of the Civil War.

Auld greeted Douglass warmly, respectfully calling him "Marshall Douglass" in honor of his new title. Douglass replied that to Thomas Auld, he would always be known just as Frederick. The two men found themselves filled with emotion. Douglass's voice choked as he spoke, and Auld's hands shook. They talked for twenty minutes. Only now did Douglass learn that he had actually been born in 1818, not 1817, as he had always thought. It was not long after this encounter that Douglass learned that Thomas Auld had died.

Several years later, Douglass returned to Maryland again, this time traveling to the old Lloyd plantation. He was met there by Edward Lloyd's son. Douglass was surprised to find that his memories of the buildings and fields remained accurate. He saw the shoemaker's shop, where he had watched an uncle of his make shoes.

Back in Washington, it was easy to see how far Douglass had come from his days as a slave under Auld. In 1878, he and Anna moved to a large farmhouse across a river from

Washington. Douglass soon purchased another fifteen acres of land close to the house.

By the time Frederick and Anna moved to their new home, Anna's health was in decline. In 1882, after more than forty years of marriage, Anna died. By the end of her life, she and Frederick had grown apart. Douglass's work had always kept him on the go, whereas Anna had never learned to read and preferred to live a private life.

Two years later, in January 1884, Douglass remarried, this time to Helen Pitts, a forty-five-year-old white woman whom he had hired as a secretary. Douglass knew that this interracial marriage might cause controversy, and he tried for some

Douglass with his second wife, Helen Pitts, (sitting), and their niece, Eva *(Courtesy of the National Park Service)*

time to keep it quiet. Even some members of Helen's family objected to the marriage, but she was an independent woman. In 1886, Douglass and Helen traveled to Europe and then Egypt. Douglass had always wanted to see Egypt. He was fascinated by the thought of seeing in person the region where Western civilization had developed. After about a year abroad, they returned home.

Even as white political leaders increasingly turned their back on the former slaves, Douglass continued to support the Republican Party, hoping to steer it to positions that would be helpful to black men and women. In many southern states, white legislators had passed laws called black codes that restricted the rights of blacks. These laws included restrictions such as preventing blacks from owning land, traveling freely, and even voting.

In the 1890s, the practice of lynching also began to increase. White mobs hanged black men, often falsely claiming that the man had attacked a white woman. Douglass grew increasingly concerned about this practice, seeing it as a return to the type of violence that had marked slavery. On January 9, 1894, Douglass gave a speech, titled "The Lessons of the Hour," in which he spoke out strongly against lynching. It was to be his last great speech. He pointed out that lynching was used not to stop crimes committed by black men, but to prevent blacks from voting and exercising their rights as citizens.

Over the next year, Douglass continued to give lectures, but his usual furious pace of travel slowed. On February 10, 1895, Douglass attended a women's rights rally. Later that night, back at home, he collapsed and died. He was buried in Mount Hope Cemetery in Washington, D.C., where his first wife, Anna, and daughter Annie had been buried.

Just a few years before, Douglass had revised his final autobiography, adding more about his early life and including an update from his life over the past decade. He also reflected on what he had witnessed during his long life.

He wrote in his last autobiography that slavery should not be forgotten, despite the fact that the last slaves and slaveholders were growing older. Soon, he wrote, there would be none left to tell the story of slavery, so it was up to him to write down what he could so that Americans would not forget this part of their history:

> I have written out my experience here, not in order to exhibit my wounds and bruises and to awaken and attract sympathy to myself personally, but as a part of the history of a profoundly interesting period in American life and progress. I have meant it to be a small individual contribution to the sum of knowledge of this special period, to be handed down to after-coming generations which may want to know what things were allowed and what prohibited; what moral, social and political relations subsisted between the different varieties of the American people down to the last quarter of the nineteenth century and by what means they were modified and changed. The time is at hand when the last American slave and the last American slaveholder will disappear behind the curtain which separates the living from the dead and when neither master nor slave will be left to tell the story of their respective relations or what happened to either in those relations. My part has been to tell the story of the slave. The story of the master never wanted for narrators.

Douglass had spent his life telling the story of the slaves and arguing that black men and women were equal to whites. The United States had always been his home, even when it had rejected his attempts to be a full citizen. In telling his story, he demanded that all Americans live up to the promises of the Founding Fathers—that all men and women be given their rights as citizens. It would be many more years before the civil rights movement fulfilled the promise of emancipation, but it might have been even longer without the tireless efforts of Frederick Douglass.

Frederick Douglass, 1879
(Courtesy of the National
Archives and Records
Administration)

# Timeline

| | |
|---|---|
| 1818 | Born a slave in eastern Maryland to Harriet Bailey, a slave; father rumored to be his white master, Aaron Anthony. |
| 1826 | Mother dies; sent to live with Hugh Auld and his wife, Sophia. |
| 1827 | Taught to read by Sophia Auld until stopped by her husband. |
| 1829–30 | Works in a shipyard. |
| 1833 | Sent to St. Michaels, Maryland, to work for Thomas Auld, Aaron Anthony's son-in-law. |
| 1834 | Rented to farmer Edward Covey; brutally beaten several times, but fights back. |
| 1836 | Jailed and released after an escape plan is discovered. |
| 1837 | Meets Anna Murray, a free black. |
| 1838 | Escapes from slavery in Baltimore to New York City; marries Anna Murray and moves to New Bedford, Massachusetts. |
| 1839 | Daughter Rosetta born. |
| 1840 | Son Lewis Henry born. |
| 1841 | Son Charles Remond born; gives first public abolitionist speech at a meeting on the island of Nantucket. |
| 1845 | Publishes an autobiography, *Narrative of the Life of Frederick Douglass;* begins a long trip to Great Britain and Ireland; English friends "buy" his freedom from Hugh Auld for $1,250. |
| 1847 | Publishes the first issue of the *North Star.* |
| 1849 | Daughter Annie born. |
| 1852 | Gives his famous "Fourth of July" speech in Rochester, New York. |

| 1859 | Implicated in slave insurrection led by John Brown to attack Harpers Ferry, Virginia; flees to Canada and then to England to escape arrest. |
| 1860 | Daughter Annie dies; returns to the United States. |
| 1861 | Civil War begins after Confederate troops fire on Fort Sumter. |
| 1863 | Becomes a recruiter for the Fifty-fourth Massachusetts Infantry; sons Lewis and Charles join the regiment; President Lincoln issues the Emancipation Proclamation on New Year's Day. |
| 1872 | Moves family to Washington, D.C., after suspicious fire destroys his Rochester home. |
| 1865 | Civil War ends; Thirteenth Amendment to the Constitution bans slavery. |
| 1877 | Appointed U.S. marshal of the District of Columbia by President Hayes. |
| 1882 | Wife of forty-six years, Anna Murray Douglass, dies. |
| 1884 | Marries Helen Pitts, his white secretary. |
| 1886–87 | Tours Europe and Africa with wife. |
| 1895 | Dies of heart failure in Washington, D.C., on February 10. |

# Sources

## Chapter One: Born into Slavery
p. 9,   "Fed, Fed . . ." Frederick Douglass, *Life and Times of Frederick Douglass* (New York: Collier Books, 1962), 33.

## Chapter Two: An Educated Slave
p. 20,   "If you teach him . . ." Douglass, *Life and Times of Frederick Douglass*, 79.
p. 22,   "I wish I could . . ." Ibid., 83.
p. 27,   "I never left . . ." Frederick Douglass, Narrative of the Life of Frederick Douglass An American Slave (Whitefish, MT: Kessinger Publishing, LLC, 2004), 43.

## Chapter Three: Fighting to Survive
p. 32,   "Covey succeeded . . ." Frederick Douglass, *Narrative of the Life of Frederick Douglass* (New York: Penguin Books, 1997), 73.

## Chapter Four: Dreaming of Freedom
p. 44,   "No, I won't! . . ." Ibid., 94.
p. 52,   "I have a great mind . . ." Frederick Douglass, *My Bondage and My Freedom* (New York: Miller, Orton, and Mulligan, 1855), 330.

## Chapter Five: Northward Bound
p. 55,   "I suppose . . ." Douglass, *Life and Times*, 199.
p. 56-57, "It was a moment . . ." Douglass, *Narrative*, 109.
p. 59,   "The people looked . . ." Ibid., 114.
p. 64,   "No! . . ." William Lloyd Garrison, preface to Douglass, *Narrative*, 5.

## Chapter Six: A New Career
p. 69,   "Prejudice against color . . ." Frederick Douglass, *The Frederick Douglass Papers, Series One: Speeches, Debates, and Interviews, Volume I: 1841-46*, John W. Blassingame, ed. (New Haven: Yale University Press, 1979), 5.
p. 69,   "Give us the facts . . ." Douglass, *Life and Times*, 217.
p. 69,   "People won't believe . . ." Ibid., 218.
p. 75,   "In thinking of America . . ." Douglass, *My Bondage and My Freedom*, 368-369.
p. 76,   "I am the representative . . ." Douglass, *Frederick Douglass Papers, Volume I*, 36.
p. 77,   "Ran away . . ." Ibid., 52.

## Chapter Eight: The Constitution Question

p. 97,   "The blessings . . ." Frederick Douglass, *The Frederick Douglass Papers, Series One: Speeches, Debates, and Interviews, Volume II: 1847-54*, John W. Blassingame, ed. (New Haven: Yale University Press, 1982), 368.

p. 97,   "What, to the American slave . . ." Ibid., 370.

p. 97,   "Must I undertake . . ." Ibid., 369.

p. 97,   "Interpreted as it ought . . ." Ibid., 385.

p. 97,   "The doom of slavery . . ." Ibid., 386-387.

p. 100,  "every man that takes part . . ." Douglass, *Frederick Douglass Papers, Volume I*, 320.

p. 102,  "The glorious doctrines . . ." Douglass, *Frederick Douglass Papers, Volume II*, 425.

p. 105,  "Men instinctively . . ." Ibid., 502.

## Chapter Nine: An Escalating Conflict

p. 109,  "It is, I think . . ." Ibid., 544.

p. 112,  "The announcement came . . ." Douglass, *Life and Times*, 307.

## Chapter Ten: An American Citizen

p. 123,  "Men fell . . ." Lewis Douglass, letter to Amelia Loguen, July 20, 1863, in *The Negro's Civil War: How American Negroes Felt and Acted during the War for the Union*, James M. McPherson, ed., (New York: Pantheon Books, 1965), 190.

p. 132,  "I have written . . ." Douglass, *Life and Times*, 478-479.

# Bibliography

Blassingame, John W., ed. *The Frederick Douglass Papers, Series One: Speeches, Debates, and Interviews, Volumes I-V.* New Haven: Yale University Press, 1979-1992.

Douglass, Frederick. *Life and Times of Frederick Douglass.* New York: Collier Books, 1962.

————.*My Bondage and My Freedom.* New York: Miller, Orton, and Mulligan, 1855.

————.*Narrative of the life of Frederick Douglass: An American Slave, Written by Himself.* New York: Penguin Books, 1997.

Kolchin, Peter. *American Slavery, 1619-1877.* New York: Hill and Wang, 1993.

Martin, Waldo E. *The Mind of Frederick Douglass.* Chapel Hill, N.C.: The University of North Carolina Press, 1984.

McFeely, William S. *Frederick Douglass.* New York: W. W. Norton & Company, 1991.

Stewart, James B. *Holy Warriors: The Abolitionists and American Slavery.* New York: Hill and Wang, 1996.

# Web sites

**http://www.pbs.org/wgbh/aia/part4/4p1539.html**
A narrative of Frederick Douglass, his 1852 "The Meaning of July Fourth for the Negro," and a letter to abolitionist William Lloyd Garrison from Harriet Beecher Stowe about their mutual friend, Douglass, are featured on this PBS site.

**http://memory.loc.gov/ammem/doughtml/doughome.html**
Here on the American Memory Project of the Library of Congress you'll find a timeline of Douglass's life, newspaper clippings of speeches he gave, and images.

**http://www.hstc.org/frederickdouglass.htm**
"Frederick Douglass: Talbot County's Native Son" is the title of an online page dedicated to Douglass by the Historical Society of Talbot County, in Easton, Maryland. The page covers everything from Douglass's early life to his rise to prominence, and contains a number of images of Douglass. The Society also describes its self-guided driving tour of fourteen sites related to Douglass's life in Talbot County.

**http://docsouth.unc.edu/neh/dougl92/menu.html**
Read the full text of the *Life and Times of Frederick Douglass, Written by Himself* on this site maintained by the University Library of the University of North Carolina at Chapel Hill. Part of its Documenting the South project, the University Library also has links to numbers of Douglass's letters and speeches.

# Photo Credits

Images on pages 11, 16, 21, 26-27, 30-31, 34-35, 106, and 135 used under license from iStockphoto.com.

Book cover and interior design by Derrick Carroll

# Index